The

CHURCH *and the*
MODERN
(1846-2005) ERA

"Telling the stories of the popes who shaped history in the modern world in *The Church and the Modern Era (1846–2005)*, David Wagner gives the reader a whirlwind tour through the encyclicals, political battles, and spiritual struggles of the successors of St. Peter. This is a book every Catholic should read, reflect on, and utilize in understanding the Catholic Church in the modern era."

Steve Weidenkopf
Author of *Timeless: A History of the Catholic Church*

"Between the election of Pope Pius IX in 1846 and the death of Pope St. John Paul II in 2005 the Church held two Vatican councils and witnessed two world wars, the rise of totalitarianism, and the sexual revolution. The same tumultuous period produced saints such as Thérèse of Lisieux, Maximilian Kolbe, and Mother Teresa of Calcutta. This well-researched, intelligently organized, reader-friendly guide makes sense of it all."

Jane Greer
Reviewer at *Angelus*
Author of *Love like a Conflagration*

"Learning about the Church's place in modern history is an incredibly fascinating endeavor and David Wagner has brought it to the popular level in his book *The Church and the Modern Era (1846–2005)*. By effortlessly weaving the facts of history with the stories of incredible saints who lived through the events themselves, Wagner has given all of us a beautiful opportunity to delve into modern history from a Catholic perspective."

Tommy Tighe
Author of *The Catholic Hipster Handbook*

"Richly documented, immensely informative, and engagingly written, David Wagner's *The Church and the Modern Era (1846–2005)* traces the story of Catholicism from the pontificate of Blessed Pius IX through the pontificate of St. John Paul II. These were the peak years of the Modern Era, when the explosive growth of scientific knowledge and technological proficiency vastly expanded the human capacity for both good and evil, while millions celebrated freedom even as they fell prey to the dictatorship of relativism. This book offers an illuminating introduction to a crucial period in which the Church faced the challenge of announcing the Good News of Jesus Christ to a befuddled world."

Russell Shaw
Author of *American Church*

The CHURCH and the MODERN ERA

(1846–2005)

Pius IX, World Wars, and the Second Vatican Council

DAVID M. WAGNER

Series Editor, Mike Aquilina

Ave Maria Press AVE Notre Dame, Indiana

≣ RECLAIMING CATHOLIC HISTORY ≣

The history of the Catholic Church is often clouded by myth, misinformation, and missing pieces. Today there is a renewed interest in recovering the true history of the Church, correcting the record in the wake of centuries of half-truths and noble lies. Books in the Reclaiming Catholic History series, edited by Mike Aquilina and written by leading authors and historians, bring Church history to life, debunking the myths one era at a time.

The Early Church
The Church and the Roman Empire
The Church and the Dark Ages
The Church and the Middle Ages
The Church and the Reformation
The Church and the Age of Enlightenment
The Church and the Modern Era

Founded in 1865, Ave Maria Press is a ministry of the United States Province of Holy Cross.

www.avemariapress.com

Paperback: ISBN-13 978-1-59471-787-1

E-book: ISBN-13 978-1-59471-788-8

Cover images © Keystone-France/Getty Images and iStock.

Cover and text design by Andy Wagoner.

Printed and bound in the United States of America.

Library of Congress Cataloging-in-Publication Data
Names: Wagner, David M. (David Mark), 1958- author.
Title: The church and the modern era (1846-2005) : Pius IX, world wars, and the Second Vatican Council / David M. Wagner.
Description: Notre Dame, Indinana : Ave Maria Press, 2020. | Series: Reclaiming Catholic history | Includes bibliographical references and index. | Summary: "The Church and the Modern Era (1846-2005) is the seventh chronological volume of the Reclaiming Catholic History series. In this exploration of the Church's most recent history, Catholic author David Wagner dispels the commonly held myths and misconceptions that color how we understand our own times, highlights the lives and contributions of modern popes and great saints, and charts the challenges the Church has faced-within and without-during this period of dramatic change"-- Provided by publisher.
Identifiers: LCCN 2020009799 (print) | LCCN 2020009800 (ebook) | ISBN 9781594717871 (paperback) | ISBN 9781594717888 (ebook)
Subjects: LCSH: Catholic Church--History. | Pius IX, Pope, 1792-1878 | Vatican Council (2nd : 1962-1965 : Basilica di San Pietro in Vaticano)
Classification: LCC BX1365 .W34 2020 (print) | LCC BX1365 (ebook) | DDC 282.09/04--dc23
LC record available at https://lccn.loc.gov/2020009799
LC ebook record available at https://lccn.loc.gov/2020009800

Contents

≡ RECLAIMING CATHOLIC HISTORY ≡
Series Introduction

"History is bunk," said the inventor Henry Ford. And he's not the only cynic to venture judgment. As long as people have been fighting wars and writing books, critics have been there to grumble because "history is what's written by the winners."

Since history had so often been corrupted by political motives, historians in recent centuries have labored to "purify" history and make it a bare science. From now on, they declared, history should record only facts, without any personal interpretation, without moralizing, without favoring any perspective at all.

It sounds like a good idea. We all want to know the facts. The problem is that it's just not possible. We cannot record history the way we tabulate results of a laboratory experiment. Why not? Because we cannot possibly record all the factors that influence a single person's action—his genetic makeup, the personalities of his parents, the circumstances of his upbringing, the climate in his native land, the state of the economy, the anxieties of his neighbors, the popular superstitions of his time, his chronic indigestion, the weather on a particular day, and the secret longings of his heart.

For any action taken in history, there is simply too much material to record, and there is so much more we do not know and can never know. Even if we were to collect data scrupulously and voluminously, we would still need to assign it relative importance. After all, was the climate more important than his genetic makeup?

But once you begin to select certain facts and leave others out—and once you begin to emphasize some details over others—you have already begun to impose your own perspective, your interpretation, and your idea of the story.

Still, there is no other way to practice history honestly. When we read, or teach, or write history, we are discerning a story line. We are saying that certain events are directly related to other events. We say that events proceed in a particular manner until they reach a particular end, and that they resolve themselves in a particular way.

Every historian has to find the principle that makes sense of those events. Some choose economics, saying that all human decisions are based on the poverty or prosperity of nations and neighborhoods, the comfort or needs of a given person or population. Other historians see history as a succession of wars and diplomatic maneuvers. But if you see history this way, you are not practicing a pure science. You are using an interpretive key that you've chosen from many possibilities but that is no less arbitrary than the one chosen in olden days, when the victors wrote the history. If you choose wars or economics, you are admitting a certain belief: that what matters most is power, wealth, and pleasure in this world. In doing so, however, you must assign a lesser role, for example, to the arts, to family life, and to religion.

But if there is a God—and most people believe there is—then God's view of things should not be merely incidental or personal. God's outlook should define objectivity. God's view should provide the objective meaning of history.

So how do we get God's view of history? Who can scale the heavens to bring God down? We can't, of course. But since God chose to come down and reveal himself and his purposes to us, we might be able to find what the Greek historians and philosophers despaired of ever finding—that is, the basis for a universal history.

The pagans knew they could not have a science without universal principles. But universal principles were elusive because no one could transcend his own culture—and no one dared to question the rightness of the regime.

Not until the Bible do we encounter histories written by historical losers. God's people were regularly defeated, enslaved, oppressed, occupied, and exiled. Yet they told their story honestly, because they held themselves—and their historians—to a higher judgment, higher even than the king or the forces of the market. They looked at history in terms of God's judgment, blessings, curses, and mercy. This became their principle of selection and interpretation of events. It didn't matter so much whether the story flattered the king or the victorious armies.

The Bible's human authors saw history in terms of covenant. In the ancient world, a covenant was the sacred and legal way that people created a family bond. Marriage was a covenant, and adoption was a covenant. And God's relationship with his people was always based on a covenant.

God's plan for the kingdom of heaven uses the kingdoms of earth. And these kingdoms are engaged by God and evangelized for his purpose. Providence harnesses the road system and the political system of the Roman Empire, and puts it all to use to advance the Gospel. Yet Rome, too, came in for divine judgment. If God did not spare the holy city of Jerusalem, then neither would Rome be exempted.

And so the pattern continued through all the subsequent thousands of years—through the rise and fall of the Byzantine Empire, the European empires, and into the new world order that exists for our own fleeting moment.

There's a danger, of course, in trying to discern God's perspective. We always run the risk of moralizing, presuming too much, or playing the prophet. There's always a danger, too, of identifying God with one "side" or another in a given war or rivalry. Christian history, at its best, transcends these problems. We can recognize that even when pagan Persia was the most vehement enemy of Christian Byzantium, the tiny Christian minority in Persia was practicing the purest and most refined Christianity the world has seen. When God uses imperial structures to advance the Gospel, the imperial structures have no monopoly on God.

It takes a subtle, discerning, and modest hand to write truly Christian history. In studying world events, a Christian historian must strive to see God's fatherly plan for the whole human race and how it has unfolded since the first Pentecost.

Christian history tells the story not of an empire, nor of a culture, but of a family. And it is a story, not a scientific treatise. In many languages, the connection is clear. In Spanish, Portuguese, Italian, and German, for example, the same word is used for "history" as for "story": *historia, história, storia, Geschichte*. In English we can lose sight of this and teach history as a succession of dates to be memorized and maps to be drawn. The timelines and atlases are certainly important, but they don't communicate to ordinary people why they should want to read history. Jacques Barzun complained, almost a half-century ago, that history had fallen out of usefulness for ordinary people and was little read. It had fragmented into overspecialized micro-disciplines, with off-putting names like "psycho-history" and "quanto-history."

The authors in this series are striving to communicate history in a way that's accessible and even entertaining. They see history as true stories well told. They don't fear humor or pathos as threats to their trustworthiness. They are unabashed about their chosen perspective, but they are neither producing propaganda nor trashing tradition. The sins and errors of Christians (even Christian saints) are an important part of the grand narrative.

The Catholic Church's story is our inheritance, our legacy, our pride and joy, and our cautionary tale. We ignore the past at our peril. We cannot see the present clearly without a deep sense of Christian history.

Mike Aquilina
Reclaiming Catholic History Series Editor

Chronology of *The Church and the Modern Era (1846–2005)*

1842	University of Notre Dame is founded by Fr. Edward Sorin, C.S.C., in South Bend, Indiana
1845–1849	Irish potato famine
1846	Election of Pius IX, longest-reigning pope
1847	Latin patriarch returns to Jerusalem
1848	Year of Revolutions; John Bosco founds the Salesians; assassination of Vatican official Count Rossi; Karl Marx publishes *The Communist Manifesto*
1850	Catholic hierarchy reestablished in England
1854	Dogma of the Immaculate Conception by Pope Pius IX
1856	Augustinian friar Gregor Mendel begins experiments that lead to fundamental laws of heredity
1858	Marian apparitions to Bernadette Soubirous at Lourdes, France
1861–1865	United States Civil War
1866	John Henry Newman completes his autobiography, *Apologia Pro Vita Sua*
1869	Pius IX opens the First Vatican Council
1870	Founding of Italy; unification of Germany; *Pastor Aeternus* proclaims the dogma of papal infallibility; Complete loss of the Papal States
1873–1875	Kulturkampf in Germany enacts laws against the Church

1878   Death of Pius IX and election of Pope Leo XIII

1890   Former Sudanese slave Bakhita is baptized Josephine Mar-
              garet Fortunata by Archbishop Giuseppe Sarto, the future
              Pope Pius X

1891   Encyclical *Rerum Novarum* is published

1897   Thérèse of Lisieux dies

1899–1901   The Boxer Rebellion occurs in China

1902   Maria Goretti is murdered

1903   Death of Leo XIII and election of Pius X; Wright brothers
              fly first airplane at Kitty Hawk, North Carolina

1914   Archduke Ferdinand's assassination in Serbia leads to
              World War I (1914–1919); death of Pius X and election of
              Pope Benedict XV

1914–1923   Armenian Genocide

1917   Russian Bolshevik Revolution; three shepherd children
              report apparitions of the Virgin Mary in Fatima, Portugal;
              first comprehensive Code of Canon Law is published

1919   Treaty of Versailles ends World War I

1920   Joan of Arc is canonized after almost five hundred years;
              Karol Wojtyła (future St. John Paul II) is born in Poland

1922   Death of Benedict XV and election of Pope Pius XI; G. K.
              Chesterton converts to Catholicism

1926–1929   Cristeros Rebellion in Mexico

1928   Josemaría Escrivá founds Opus Dei

1929   Vatican City State is established by the Lateran Treaty with
              Italy

1932–1933	Ukrainian Genocide; man-made famine imposed by Stalin's regime
1933	Rise of Adolph Hitler and the Nazi Party in Germany; concordat between the Holy See and Germany signed; Dorothy Day and Peter Maurin found *Catholic Worker*
1937	Pius XI issues *Mitt Brennender Sorge* (*On the Church and the German Reich*)
1939	Death of Pius XI and election of Pius XII; Germany invades Poland, beginning World War II (1939–1945)
1941	Maximilian Kolbe is executed at Auschwitz; Teresa Benedicta of the Cross (Edith Stein) is killed one year later
1944	Rome occupied by German Army; D-Day
1945	World War II ends in Europe; first atomic bombs used against Japan end the war in the Pacific
1945–1949	Chinese Communist revolution led by Mao Zedong
1945–1960	Decolonization of Asia and Africa
1948	State of Israel is founded
1950	Dogma of the assumption of Mary declared by Pius XII in *Munificentissimus Deus*
1952	Elizabeth II is crowned Queen of England
1958	Death of Pius XII and election of John XXIII
1960	John F. Kennedy is elected the first Catholic president of the United States
1962	Second Vatican Council opened by John XXIII
1963	Death of John XXIII and election of Paul VI, the last pope to wear the papal triple tiara
1965	Vatican II closes

1968   Paul VI publishes *Humanae Vitae*

1969   First man lands on the moon

1978   The Year of Three Popes: death of Paul VI and election of Pope John Paul I; death of John Paul I and election of John Paul II

1979   Pope John Paul II visits his homeland, communist Poland, for nine days

1980   Archbishop Oscar Romero assassinated in El Salvador

1981   Attempt to assassinate Pope John Paul II fails on the Feast of Our Lady of Fatima

1984   First World Youth Day

1989   Berlin Wall is destroyed and the "iron curtain" of communism in Europe falls

1991   Collapse of the Soviet Union

1992   *Catechism of the Catholic Church* published

1997   England's Princess Diana dies in a car accident; Missionaries of Charity founder Mother Teresa dies a few days later in Kolkata, India

2000   Jubilee Year as the Church enters its third millennium

2001–2002   The *Boston Globe* investigates clergy sexual abuse and subsequent coverup by church leaders

2005   Death of Fatima visionary Carmelite Sister Lucia; death of John Paul II and election of Pope Benedict XVI

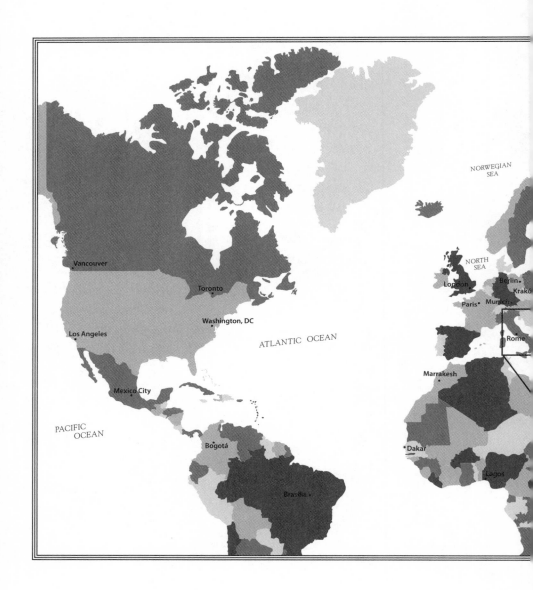

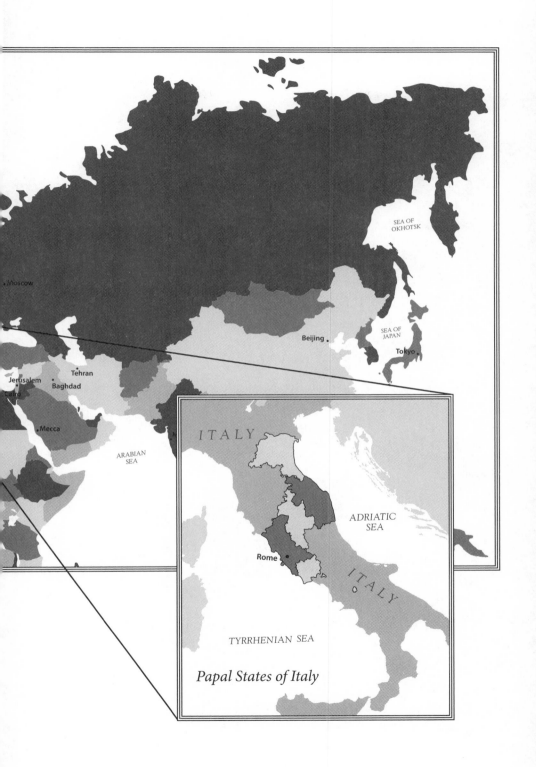

Papal States of Italy

When Does Something Become "History"?

Hindsight is twenty-twenty.

When we hear the word *history*, most of us imagine people and events in the distant past—those the vast majority of people now alive cannot personally recall. While we certainly lose the detail that accompanies proximity, distance enables us to see events in the light of their consequences. Following a thread back from where we are, we can uncover the broader context of where it led. As a result, we tend to judge history by a perspective that could never have been available to the people who lived and shaped it. Hindsight may be twenty-twenty, but it's safe to say that most of us see our own times quite myopically. When things are near, we tend to interpret them personally.

Objects in mirror are closer than they appear.

The Church and the Modern Era comes dangerously close to being a book about things many of us still remember. Perhaps that is why it has been a bit tricky to write. All news eventually becomes "history." But it's hard to say just when (or even how) that occurs, because the line between current events and history is rarely clear; nor is it written in stone. For most of us, the nineteenth century feels like history; the end of the twentieth does not. Some of the events recounted here are still "current." Others—such as the loss of the Papal States or the dogma of the assumption—are certainly closer to us than they appear when we look back.

This volume of the Reclaiming Catholic History series will examine the most recent period of Church history. If we do so through a wide-angle lens, beginning with the election of Bl. Pius IX in 1846 and ending with the death of St. John Paul II in 2005, it becomes clear that we have crossed into a new era of Church history and left the modern era behind. Whether our times are "postmodern," "post-Christian," or something else remains to be seen.

You may well ask, why begin at 1846? After all, so little of what we'd call "modern" existed, even though modernization was well underway. By 1846, the French Revolution was over, Napoleon was dead, and North America had mostly severed ties with Europe. Amid the chaos and instability that ensued, something new was emerging. Absolute monarchies were falling, nation-states were rising, and industrialization and mass migration had begun. It is unlikely that the cardinals who gathered at the conclave of 1846 knew that they were choosing the "first modern pope," but that is how Bl. Pius IX, the longest-reigning pope other than St. Peter, has come to be known.

On the other end, one might wonder if 2005 really marks the end of an era. Why not the close of Vatican II in 1965, the year 2000, or the election of Pope Francis in 2013? And that is where the question about when something becomes history bounces back at us. The line between eras is not hard and fast. Events, trends, and people cross any lines we might try to draw. That being said, there are reasons to choose 2005 as an ending point for the modern era. St. John Paul II is the last pope who served as a Council Father at Vatican II. His pontificate focused on evangelization, and the third millennium opened the doors to the future and carried the whole Church, as it were, over the threshold. His death in 2005, forty years after the close of the Second Vatican Council, is arguably the cleanest place to end.

Anyone who explores the Church in this period cannot help but notice the importance of Peter's successors and their influence on both Church history and world events. I have structured this book largely around their pontificates. Many, perhaps a disproportionate number, of these popes were extraordinarily holy men. As other volumes in this series will certainly show, that is not always the case. We stand at the end of a long line of canonized popes. Of the ten popes covered in this book, four are saints, one is blessed, and two are venerable. As for Leo XIII, Benedict XV, and Pius XI, serious arguments for their extraordinary sanctity are available.

It is also important to note that while the world we live in has arguably changed more in this period than in any previous era, the faith has not. On the surface, the Church may look and feel more "user-friendly" and less "formal" than ever. But what we believe has been handed down to us, as it has been from the beginning. Our challenges are largely the same as those faced by disciples in every age: to live the fullness of the faith we have received as the Church of Jesus Christ.

Chapter 1

The Modern Church

A man jumped from the crowd—a knife shimmered. Count Rossi's scream was loud, but brief. The pope's friend and now political colleague was suddenly on the ground, dying, stabbed with a dagger in the neck as he ascended the assembly hall stairs to present his plan for a new constitutional order. Rossi had been warned. The anger was tangible ever since Pius IX had withdrawn the papal army from the First Italian War of Independence. Violence had broken out in the streets of Rome, and Count Rossi had been declared an enemy of the people. That's why none of the Civic Guards who witnessed his murder in the courtyard made any attempt to arrest the killer. Whatever His Holiness might say, it was necessary to get him out of Rome. Thankfully, the King of the Two Sicilies had offered him refuge. Pius escaped to Gaeta, about seventy-five miles south, disguised as an ordinary priest.

Giving government addresses to a papal parliament was not something popes or their assistants were used to doing. For centuries popes had governed their territory as monarchs, gaining vital protection for the Church against hostile kings, dukes, and nations. But when Giovanni-Maria Mastai-Ferretti was elected Pope Pius IX in 1846, the world around him was moving toward parliamentary governments.

The world was changing fast, in ways both good and bad. The sobriquet "first modern pope" has been applied to various popes of the recent and not-so-recent past. Pius IX probably deserves it most, though he would have wanted it least. During his pontificate, Europe was utterly transformed.

In 1846, the Church had a predominantly European focus (though this was beginning to change); Europe was a patchwork of small states, many of them with long traditions tying Catholicism to their government and nationhood, but also some with a recent record of anti-religious revolution.

France had been affectionately called "the eldest daughter of the Church." During the French Revolution, however, many had become hostile to God; practicing Catholics were exterminated, and an actress dressed up as "the goddess Reason" was installed in Paris's Cathedral of Notre Dame. While the anti-Christian fervor of revolutionary France was supposedly reversed with the Restoration of 1815–1830, aftershocks of the "revolution" were still echoing all over Europe when Pius IX was elected.

Besides nations tottering between old Catholic loyalties and the revolution, the Papal States added further complication. A more-than-millennium-old territorial jurisdiction in central Italy, the Papal States was governed temporally as well as spiritually by the pope. While its territory varied in size from its beginning in 754 until 1870, it had always included Rome, numerous surrounding cities, and stretched across Italy from sea to sea.

Liberalism and the Revolution

The political vocabulary of this era is inconsistent and confusing. The French Revolution was based on principles that are historically part of classical liberalism—liberty, equality, fraternity, and hallmarks of the "social contract"—but it turned violent, collectively oriented, and statist very quickly. Once France's religious and political traditions were abruptly repudiated and consigned to a past that was deemed entirely evil, many leaders became convinced that everyone who disagreed must be eliminated as an "enemy of the people." The quick descent to the Reign of Terror was noted all over Europe by Catholics as well as by those we might call political conservatives.

As pope, Pius had released many people imprisoned for dissent and initiated improvements in the prisons of the Papal States. He also ended a practice of mandating that Jews in Rome listen to a Catholic homily every week. Even with reforms that had European political salons talking about a "liberal pope," the "revolution" had put down roots in the more remote parts of the Papal States. By 1848 it had reached Rome, through the influence of Italian nationalist leaders such as Garibaldi and Mazzini. Garibaldi was a leader of a Masonic paramilitary force called the Carabinieri. Mazzini was an intellectual who envisioned the pope named the "President of Italy."

To be both pope and "president" of a united Italy would take the papacy's temporal power further than Pius thought it should go. The Papal States were one thing; it would be something else to govern all the way from the southern Alps down to Sicily, not as political custodian of a spiritual patrimony, but as a political leader. Perhaps worse—it would have tied the papacy even more tightly to Italy than it already was. The papacy is, after all, universal. The pope is Patriarch of the West, Successor of St. Peter, Pontifex Maximus, Servant of the Servants of God, and Vicar of Christ. How could he, at the same time, be President of Italy?

When revolutionary forces gained power in Rome early in 1848, Pius could have relied on the power of Austria to rescue him and the Papal States. But he did not want to invite troops of a foreign nation to fire on "his" people, people for whom he had temporal as well as spiritual responsibility, people who might be rebelling against real injustices and not against God.

So he agreed that the Papal States should move toward parliamentary government. The goals of the revolutionary liberals went far beyond parliamentarianism and even against it, but as of 1848, setting up a parliament and holding elections for it was a liberal step, Pius IX thought, and was reasonable and nonthreatening to the Church.

That is what brought Count Rossi to the parliament in November 1848. Pius trusted Rossi and thought the people of Rome would also trust him, but their mood had changed in the two years Pius had been pope, notwithstanding his reforms. Evenings in the courtyard of the Quirinal Palace, when the newly elected pontiff had met with crowds who acclaimed him, now seemed distant. Many who had shared them expected this new pope would lend himself to the project most dear to the liberalism of that period: the unification of Italy. But despite his duties as monarch of the

Papal States, Pius saw his mission as almost purely spiritual. That is why he proposed not only a parliament but also a set of officials to run the secular side of papal government. At the head of these was Count Rossi. Thus we arrive where we began, in November 1848: with Pius IX's hopes for constitutional liberalism in the Papal States getting their throat cut in the person of Count Rossi.

By 1850 Pius was back in Rome, thanks to help from an unlikely source: not Austria, but France—now under the influence of a new president: Louis-Napoleon Bonaparte, nephew of the "Emperor," Napoleon I. The nephew was not without ambition—he would shortly "crown" himself as Napoleon III. Surely conflict lay in the future between Napoleon III's empire and the Papal States. But for now, Louis-Napoleon remembered that as a bishop, the future Pius IX had been generous to him when he was taken prisoner in an uprising, so he returned the favor.

Restoration of the English Hierarchy

When Henry VIII made himself the head of the church in England in the 1530s, he took all the sees and bishoprics that the Catholic Church had founded, going back to St. Augustine of Canterbury in the sixth century. As a result, Canterbury was no longer the senior diocese of the Catholic Church in England, but rather that of a new church that no longer recognized the authority of the pope.

After three hundred years, two things had become clear: (1) between Catholic emancipation, Irish immigration as a result of the potato famine, and the wave of intellectual converts inspired by St. John Henry Newman, the Catholic population in Britain was growing; and (2) the Church of England was not about to apologize, or give back all those dioceses, cathedrals, and churches, any time soon.

Catholics in Britain had vicars apostolic instead of bishops. One of them, Fr. Nicholas Wiseman, visited Pope Pius in 1847 to promote the idea of a restored hierarchy. The pope agreed in principle, but in the midst of the other troubles going on in Rome, the idea did not make immediate headway.

Once he returned to Rome, Pius published a Bull of Restoration on September 30, 1850, and on October 7, Cardinal Wiseman issued his own pastoral letter, *From Out of the Flaminian Gate*. The English were not pleased. Since Pius's forced flight from Rome and the defeat of the (most recent) Roman Republic, many Italian nationalists had washed up in London with their version of current events. Instead of a reforming pontiff besieged by shabby revolutionaries, London society now saw underdog freedom fighters right out of their Latin textbooks, confronting that traditional English villain—the pope.

So Parliament enacted a law that made it a crime to do something that Pius had already decided *not* to do: duplicate the diocesan names of the Church of England. There would be no new Catholic Archbishop of Canterbury or London: those had both become Anglican titles. Westminster, however, was a name drenched in English political and religious history, but it had no diocese. The principal see of the restored English Catholic hierarchy could be called the Archdiocese of Westminster, with its Westminster Cathedral (near Victoria Station), and Cardinal Wiseman as archbishop.

The Immaculate Conception

Since at least the Middle Ages, Christians have believed in the Immaculate Conception, that is, that the Virgin Mary was preserved from original sin. By the nineteenth century, more and more bishops were requesting that it be defined as a dogma.

In the thirteenth century, the idea of Mary being "free from" original sin aroused controversy. Some argued that Mary had no need whatsoever of the redemption wrought by Christ. Other theologians objected, reasonably, that this would be an unsupported exception to Romans 3:23 ("since all have sinned and fall short of the glory of God"). But a more fully considered version of the Immaculate Conception was available: Mary, too, needed Christ's redemption, but God had granted her a share of it at the moment of her conception so that she would be an unstained passageway for Christ into the human world at the Incarnation.

God did not, of course, need a *physically* clean space: that's why he was born in a manger, not a palace. But to clear himself a space free from original sin? This was something fitting; it was also within God's power. Because God lives outside the limitations of time, the fruits of the Cross and Resurrection could be applied from eternity either before or after the events occurred in history.

Pius's and the Church's official definition and proclamation of the Immaculate Conception reads as follows:

> We declare, pronounce, and define that the doctrine which holds that the most Blessed Virgin Mary, in the first instance of her conception, by a singular grace and privilege granted by Almighty God, in view of the merits of Jesus Christ, the Savior of the human race, was preserved free from all stain of original sin, is a doctrine revealed by God and therefore to be believed firmly and constantly by all the faithful.[1]

This declaration goes over the whole history of the doctrine.

On the Wrong Side of History: The Mortara Case

In 1858, there occurred an unjust act for which Pius IX was responsible— for which he took responsibility, but which he also believed was necessary and even good. A six-year-old boy, Edgardo Mortara, whose Jewish family lived within the Papal States, was taken from his family by papal marshals. This action was taken because the child had been surreptitiously baptized as an infant by the family's teenaged Catholic housekeeper when he had been sick and in danger of death.

According to Catholic teaching as interpreted by Pius in this case (and this is not a binding magisterial interpretation), Baptism gave Edgardo the right to a Catholic upbringing, and gave the Church—at least in the Papal States, where the Pope was political ruler as well as ecclesiastical leader—a duty to see that he got one.

Some negotiations ensued (or even preceded Edgardo's seizure, according to Edgardo's memoir, but there are grounds to believe he was mistaken on this point), in which the Papal side floated options that might have kept contact between Edgardo and his parents. But understandably, these options—such as sending Edgardo to a Jesuit school nearby—were not acceptable to his Jewish parents. It is also understandable that his parents were grief-stricken and viewed the boy's removal as an act of tyranny.

Pius took heavy criticism in the international press, but stood by his view that he could not do otherwise. He also made Edgardo his own godson and took a direct interest in his further upbringing, but this is as likely to be seen as exacerbating the situation as mitigating it.

Further facts—that Edgardo eventually became a priest, took the name "Pius," and wrote a memoir in which he expressed great regard for Pius IX and desire to see him canonized—add further complications. But even when all the background is brought to bear, we must still consider this incident a stain on the character of an otherwise good pope.

Here is some of that background.

Forcibly or surreptitiously baptizing children against the wishes of their parents has always been against Church doctrine and policy, as far as records show. In fact, Catholics in the nineteenth century Papal States were discouraged from taking jobs in Jewish households, not (or not *only*) because of anti-Semitism, but to avoid temptations to carry out such baptisms as the Mortaras' young Catholic housekeeper had carried out on Edgardo.

St. Thomas Aquinas taught that children of non-Christians should not be baptized against the wishes of their parents because of parents' rights under natural law to raise their own children. Most observers, including most Catholic ones, agree that Pius's actions were contrary to Aquinas's teaching on this matter. This is not beyond dispute, however, because Aquinas did not discuss the specific case of a baptized child living in a non-Christian family.

Pius thought this case was different because Edgardo's baptism had not been a mere subterfuge to get around his parents' right to raise him as they wished. Rather, it had been carried out when Edgardo, as a baby, had been very ill and near death. Yet he recovered, and the fact that he had been baptized eventually became known.

Before we wag our twenty-first century fingers, however, we should acknowledge that it is the approved practice of governments in the U.S. and western Europe to take children away from their parents when abuse or neglect is occuring in the home—and also, much more controversially, when abuse or neglect is merely suspected.

In other words, we cannot claim that we ourselves believe no child should ever be taken from his or her parents. Instead, we conclude that Pius did not have an adequate reason. Of course, people who don't believe in Catholicism or the efficacy of Baptism will believe Pius had no reason at all and therefore acted with extreme tyranny. Those who do believe in these things will mostly concur that he acted wrongly, but may mitigate his guilt to a greater or lesser extent.

Interestingly, the governments that officially condemned Pius at the time did not have clean hands. Britain, for instance, had no qualms about an alliance with the Ottoman Empire as a counterweight to the growing and feared power of Russia. At that time, it was Ottoman policy and practice to take children from Christian families and raise them as Muslims and as ultra-loyal guards to the Sultan, called Janissaries, or else to castrate them and raise them as court eunuchs.

In other words, shining a light equally into Pius's world and our own rips away the soothing illusion that we have things basically on track and certain isolated, terrible injustices need only be protested when they are committed by an authority that is already considered a defendant at the bar of history, such as the papacy.

But if we consider these things in order to mitigate Pius's guilt, we also have to ask: was there a consistent policy within the Papal States of taking custody of baptized children from parents who were unlikely to give them a Catholic upbringing? The (rare) Protestants in the Papal States? Notorious Catholic parents? As far as we know there was not. So the deeper question arises: were Jews targeted? But if they were, why was there only one Mortara case? (No one has claimed to have found others.)

These questions will remain unanswered. We may, however, gain a few takeaways from the Mortara case:

- Even saints and blesseds do bad things.
- The papacy's loss of temporal jurisdiction over a large territory in 1870 may have been a good thing, even though it was not seen that way by Pius IX or later popes.
- The Church teaches that all parents—not only Catholic or other Christian parents—have a right under natural law to raise their children and direct their upbringing. That is as it should be.

Error? It's in the Syllabus

By the time Pius IX felt ready to issue a compendium of warnings, the idea was not new. It was first proposed in 1849, during Pius's exile in Gaeta, by the future Pope Leo XIII. *The Syllabus of Errors* covers a variety of propositions that were coming into vogue at the time, ideas that threatened the Catholic Church and faith. Despite the *Syllabus*'s reputation in pop history as the high-water mark of papal arrogance and ignorance, Pius includes some things that are hard to understand because we lack the context in which they were first delivered.

Many of the condemnations seem to stress one word when it's another word that carries the freight. Consider number 15: "Every man is free to embrace and profess that religion which, guided by the light of reason, he shall consider true." How can that be an "error"? Because the operative word is "reason," not "free to embrace and profess." Reason is on a high pedestal, up there with revelation, in Catholic theology, but the two have to work together. Revelation without reason gives you "fideism," the error of believing without having the slightest idea why. But reason without revelation leaves us incapable of seeing—and acting on—the most important things, which are revealed.

Some of the errors can and should be proclaimed as such today, even more than in Pius IX's time. Numbers 33 and 44 foresee and condemn attempts by the state to dictate to the Church even in matters of the Church's doctrine. Number 33 says it is an error to believe that the power to direct the teaching of theological questions *does not* belong exclusively to the Church. Who was saying otherwise? Chancellor Bismarck was doing so in the parts of Germany he controlled. He was preparing an anti-Catholic policy known as the *Kulturkampf*, or the Culture Wars (perhaps the first use of the term in history). In 1863, Munich, the capital of heavily Catholic Bavaria, was not yet united with Prussia, where Bismarck was chancellor. In fact, it was negotiating with Austria for a (Catholic) alliance against (Protestant) Prussia. But Bavarians could not but be aware of Bismarck's ominous preoccupation with Catholicism as a rival for state power.)

The most famous and most derided part of the *Syllabus* is its last error listed, number 80. This one says it is an error to maintain that "the Roman Pontiff can, and ought to, reconcile himself, and come to terms with progress, liberalism and modern civilization." The thrust of this was to distinguish true from false civilization, to remind people of the Church's contributions to the former, and then to state the obvious: if "progress" and "civilization" are defined as the active de-Christianization of society, the world is going to find the pope among its opposition. Number 80 is the *Syllabus* error most often read out to students for kicks and giggles. Yet as we look back from where we are today, it may be the one that needs no defense at all.

Vatican I

There had been no ecumenical council since Trent in the sixteenth century. Then a council bishop might expect to be away from his diocese for years. Travel from very far away was largely impossible. But Pius had been smart to reverse Gregory XVI's prohibition on railroads in the Papal States, and in the 1860s, many could travel by train and get to Rome in a reasonable period of time. In the late 1860s, Pius IX became convinced that the time had come to take a doctrine already generally accepted within the Church—the infallibility of the pope on matters of faith and morals—and make it the subject of a conciliar definition.

The council would be held at the Vatican: it was by far the safest place, even though the Kingdom of Italy was ready to close in on the city if ever, and as soon as, French troops were withdrawn. This meant it would be the Vatican Council, though today we are likely to call it Vatican I. That no ecumenical council[2] had ever before been held at the Vatican may seem surprising, but remember that the St. Peter's we think of wasn't completed until 1626. Councils held in Rome took place at St. John Lateran, the "pope's cathedral" and seat as bishop of Rome. Still, Vatican I was the Church's first truly global council. Bishops attended from all over the world and from every continent.

Very few Catholic leaders did *not* already believe in such infallibility. The split of opinion, both at the council and outside it, was between advocates of a doctrinal proclamation (Infallibists) and those who argued that such a definition would be "inopportune" (the Inopportunists).

In retrospect it is easy to suspect the Inopportunists of being secret deniers of papal infallibility. After all, what made 1869 so particularly "inopportune"? What would "opportune" look like? Some Inopportunists, however, were Catholics of extreme fervor and intellectual integrity who put forth a good argument: John Henry Newman for instance. He wrote to his bishop, "When has [the] definition of doctrine *de fide* been a luxury of devotion and not a stern painful necessity?"[3] He was as Infallibist as anyone, he maintained, but his point was that if there are other good Catholics who aren't sure about infallibility, why burden their consciences if not strictly necessary?

Certainly, the Church would have survived without the definition of the Immaculate Conception and without the *Syllabus of Errors*. But then the world would have gone hurtling along its secularizing ways without the Catholic Church there to signal relief and propose an alternative. We've already seen why Pius IX was, without wanting to be, the "first modern pope": not because he asked modernity what it wanted and then made the Church conform, but because, in the face of rapid and not always wholesome change, he did the radical opposite, and did it often.

Vatican I enacted two documents before it adjourned because of the advancing Italian army. Its first constitution was *Dei Filius (Dogmatic Constitution on the Catholic Faith)*. It is noteworthy for declaring, at the conciliar level, that the existence of a creator-God, separate from his creation, can be known by reason alone. These definitions were important because a crisis of faith was sweeping Europe, and some Catholic theologians were trying to meet it on the subjective, experiential ground advocated by Protestants. The council then turned to *Pastor Aeternus*, the First Dogmatic Constitution on the Church of Christ, in which we find the solemn definitional declaration on papal infallibility.

At the council, speeches were given on both sides. The Infallibilists always had the majority. The very fact that the Inopportunists spoke out freely is taken by some anti-Catholics as proof *against* infallibility. The council voted for *Pastor Aeternus*, including this language:

> 8. But since in this very age when the salutary effectiveness of the apostolic office is most especially needed, not a few are to be found who disparage its authority, we judge it absolutely necessary to affirm solemnly the prerogative which the only-begotten Son of God was pleased to attach to the supreme pastoral office.
>
> 9. Therefore, faithfully adhering to the tradition received from the beginning of the Christian faith . . . we teach and define as a divinely revealed dogma that when the Roman Pontiff speaks EX CATHEDRA, that is, when, in the exercise of his office as shepherd and teacher of all Christians, in virtue of his supreme apostolic authority, he defines a doctrine concerning faith or morals to be held by the whole Church, he possesses, by the divine assistance promised to him in blessed Peter, that infallibility which the divine Redeemer willed his Church to enjoy in defining doctrine concerning faith or morals. Therefore, such definitions of the Roman Pontiff are of themselves, and not by the consent of the Church, irreformable."[4]

Most bishops were delighted. Most of the Inopportunists managed both to stand their ground for a decent interval and then to declare fealty.

Up Close and Personal:
ST. JOHN HENRY NEWMAN

St. John Henry Newman, canonized in 2019, was a prolific writer and the most influential English-speaking theologian of the nineteenth century. Born in London in 1801, Newman spent the first half of his life as an Anglican and the second as a Catholic. As an Anglican priest, Newman served as the vicar of Saint Mary's University Church at Oxford and was drawn to the rich and solemn high-church liturgical tradition of Anglicanism. Consequently, he became an active force in what is commonly called the Oxford Movement, whose members emphasized the importance of the Church Fathers as teachers as well as the continuity of the faith across the centuries. He would later say that "to be deep in history is to cease to be a Protestant."

While many are said to have read their way into Catholicism, Newman wrote his way into the Church and became Catholic in 1845. His conversion was highly controversial, and he lost many friendships and professional relationships over it. He was ordained a Catholic priest two years later. Though he believed in papal infallibility, Newman voiced reservations about Pius IX promulgating the dogma in 1870. Pope Leo XIII recognized Newman's great contributions to the status of the Church in England and appointed him to the College of Cardinals in 1879, even though he was neither a bishop nor a resident of Rome.

A New Fall of Rome?

Between July and September of 1870, Prussia's invasion of France (by which Bismarck would end up unifying Germany) forced Napoleon III to withdraw his forces from Rome. On September 20, the armies of the Kingdom of Italy—that growing political entity that had been built out of the Kingdom of Sardinia-Piedmont—invaded and put an end to the Papal States. The council adjourned, theoretically planning to reconvene at some point. That the Council Fathers were not hindered in their departure was one sign that the Kingdom of Italy did not plan to annihilate the papacy. Out of concern for appearances, some sort of respect, or by divine intervention, the kingdom's policy toward the pope and the Vatican was conciliatory.

But this did not extend to all of papal Rome. Churches, monasteries, and convents were closed. Taking Rome as its new capital, Italy needed an appropriate palace for its government headquarters. It chose the Quirinal Palace, which was then home to many elderly monks and nuns. In addition, priests who ventured into Rome outside the Vatican were subject to daily hostility, sometimes from "demonstrators" whom the new government could not control—or didn't want to.

The papacy's right to territory had just been extinguished for the first time in over a millennium, and an outcome that Pius had devoted much of his pontificate to trying to prevent had just happened. Unless the kingdom killed him, his next move was not obvious—except for one thing: keep running the Church.

The kingdom steered a middle course: not only generosity and protection—by its army and police if necessary—toward the pope and the sites important to the governance of the Church (e.g., St. John Lateran as well as the Vatican) but also (as we have just seen) aggressive secularization elsewhere in the city.

The government enacted a significant statute in 1871—the Law of Guarantees. By this it restrained itself from attacking the pope, the Vatican, or other papally significant sites, and also offered the pope substantial financial recompense for the losses he incurred in the taking of what had been his city. Pius refused the money and did not recognize the Law of Guarantees. If this seems arrogant, consider that what government gives, government can take away. Pius was not going to treat the powers and immunities that were his by right as if they were gifts from the king of Italy.

Pro- and Anti-Pope

In 1874 a large Catholic crowd gathered in St. Peter's to celebrate the twentieth anniversary of the declaration on the Immaculate Conception. The problem with large gatherings anywhere in post-papal, newly royal Italy was that they usually turned into demonstrations. This one did, with cries of "Long live the pope-king!" So the next day, about three hundred secularists invaded the Vatican. In keeping with its promises under the Law of Guarantees, Italy sent in some gentlemen with large rifles and bayonets who persuaded the demonstrators to desist and disperse. Outside of legally protected terrain, however, the government rarely interfered with anti-papal violence.

In Germany, Bismarck's Kulturkampf took a toll on the Church. As he saw it, North Prussian Protestantism was a necessary social unifying force for his newly united empire. So on went the church closings, the monastic expulsions, the defenses of Church teachers who openly defied the Vatican on infallibility, the denial to bishops of the right to occupy their sees, and so forth. When the government began jailing bishops, the pace and size of Catholic demonstrations picked up, especially in German Poland. Bismarck figured out this was a losing game and began unwinding the anti-Church measures, blaming them on advisers. Throughout this, Pius IX maintained an intense war of words with Germany; whether this helped the Church there or not is unclear, but Bismarck did slow down the Kulturkampf while Pius was still alive.

A King and a Pope Close an Era

After so many years representing opposing visions for an ideal Europe, King Victor Emmanuel II and Pope Pius IX died in early 1878. The king went first. He had been excommunicated, but Pius encouraged the priest attending him to hear his confession. Victor Emmanuel expressed sorrow for having caused grief to the Church, and filial loyalty to the pope. He received absolution, extreme unction, and viaticum, amid a candlelight gathering of senior courtiers.

Pius died a month later at the age of eighty-five. He was buried at first at the Vatican, but his will requested burial in a church just outside the gates of Rome, one originally built by Constantine. Gangs of "demonstrators" attacked the cortege as it was crossing the very first bridge over the Tiber and almost threw the casket into the river. The government intervened, and the cortege reached its destination. The government did well for its international reputation in this case, because even in countries that did not care for the papacy, street toughs shouting revolutionary slogans and attempting to desecrate a corpse were even less popular.

Pius IX did not respond perfectly to all of the challenges he faced; no pope could have. This is why the Church teaches that popes, though infallible in their formal, solemn teaching on faith and morals, are not beyond error in every decision. While he eschewed the temporal power of the papacy and lost the Papal States, he strengthened the pope's spiritual leadership and his role as pastor of the universal Church.

YOU BE THE JUDGE:

Wasn't the declaration of papal infallibility just a power grab?

All opponents (and some friends!) of the infallibility definition saw it as self-aggrandizement by the pope. A little thought, though, may make us wonder why this was so. In fact, infallibility was and is a *restraint* on the papacy as an institution.

In Evelyn Waugh's *Brideshead Revisited*, we are treated to a scene in which a pious Jesuit who works a lot with potential converts reports back to the equally pious Lady Marchmain about his strange failures with Rex Mottram. Mottram is a politician whose real problem as a convert is that he doesn't want to be a Catholic—he just wants cardinals in red robes at his wedding. He doesn't take the doctrine he's learning seriously—and he seems not to think anyone else does either. To Mottram it's just a matter of rote answers; he cares about pleasing Fr. Mowbray, because that means the instruction ordeal will be over sooner, but getting catechetical questions right as matters of *fact* is the furthest thing from his mind. (All quotations from Evelyn Waugh, *Brideshead Revisited*, New York: Back Bay Books/Little, Brown & Co., 1944, repr. 2012, p. 221.)

One day, Fr. Mowbray tells us, they were talking about papal power, and he asked Rex, "Supposing the Pope looked up and saw a cloud and said 'It's going to rain,' would that be bound to happen?"

Rex: "Oh yes, Father!"

Father was not prepared for this depth of ignorant sycophancy, so he moved the obvious next piece on the board—obvious to everyone but Rex, that is.

"But supposing it didn't?"

We don't need to explore how Rex digs himself deeper into the hole he's already in. The point is, *everyone knows* that papal infallibility does not extend to predicting or decreeing the weather.

Or do they? To scan the reactions of certain terrified European statesmen in the wake of *Pastor Aeternus*, one would think they took infallibility to be just the sort of wizardly omniscience, or even power over physical reality, that Rex pretends to think it is. Even worse, if they didn't think it was that, they expected their Catholic citizens would think it was, and doubt their own ability as statesmen to make their work keep up with that of the wizard.

But many critics missed the even bigger picture. Not only does papal infallibility not extend to all sorts of matters, but also it actually limits, not to say annihilates, papal power in those areas to which it does extend, once it has been used.

Consider Pius IX's 1854 decree on the Immaculate Conception. It meets all the criteria of infallibility in *Pastor Aeternus*. What *now* is the power of a later pope with regard to the doctrine of the Immaculate Conception? *Absolutely none.* It has been defined—infallibly—down to the last detail that might pertain to it.

It's a principle of all republics with lawmaking bodies (e.g. Britain's Parliament and our Congress) that one Parliament or Congress cannot bind future ones. Congress makes a law, the president signs it, and it's a law. Then there's an election, there's a sweeping change of party control, and the next Congress overturns that law, and the new president signs the bill that overturns it. The former law is gone. No parliament can, with any binding effect, forbid its successors (the one after later elections) from changing the law. It can't even forbid *itself* from changing the law, should its mind change before the next election. Legislative bodies (chosen by the people) are free and powerful.

Papal infallibility is not like that. An infallible pronouncement by a pope, on a question within the scope of infallibility, closes the possibility of change on that question *forever.* That is quite a constraint on a future pope who wants to reopen it. Pius IX and Vatican I declared a power of the papacy—and also a concomitant and severe limit on that power. The papacy does not work like parliaments, or congresses, or other merely human institutions.

Chapter 2

Democracy and the "Social Question"

At the end of Bl. Pius IX's historically long thirty-two-year reign, the cardinals gambled on an older candidate, to ensure a much briefer pontificate. They lost. Cardinal Gioacchino Pecci was sixty-eight when he took the name Leo XIII, but he still reigned for twenty-five years.

As the reserved Leo took the helm from the confrontational Pius, the Church had not fully accepted the loss of the Papal States. Pope Leo believed the Church needed *some* territory again and was interested in working with "the powers," that is, other governments in Europe to gain territory in some way. The Kingdom of Italy was unlikely to make any reliable concessions unless the Holy See was a respected international entity.

Before 1870, nuncios were papal ambassadors, emissaries of *a government*. Without territory, a state to represent, what would nuncios do except interfere with archbishops? That was the view of London's Cardinal Manning, Archbishop of Westminster, and it was shared by Irish bishops who feared a nuncio based in London would be too influenced by the Protestant establishment. Leo decided to retain the system of nuncios anyway, and objections subsided.

He dealt similarly with Bismarck's Kulturkampf ("culture war") against the Church. Bismarck's real aim was to ensure a high level of German cultural unity. The chancellor was willing to deal with a pope who showed him respect, albeit slowly. Leo showed him numerous courtesies, and one by one, the restrictions on the Church fell away. Only one restriction remained in the long term: Jesuits were not readmitted to Germany until 1917.

In dealing with France, Pope Leo made some adjustments to how Catholics should deal with adverse governments. The memory of the brutal reign of the Paris Commune, which seized power in the chaos following France's defeat by Germany in the Franco-Prussian War (1870–1871)[1], was fresh. The "communards" were filled with hate for the Church. During their brief time in power in the spring of 1871, there were martyrs. The Archbishop of Paris, Georges Darboy, the pastor of a major parish, a priest who tended the wounded during the German siege, and others noteworthy for service to Church and state were executed on May 24, 1871. Several Dominicans were shot the following day, and several Jesuits the day after that—even as the Commune was on the verge of being suppressed.[2]

France's Third Republic (1871–1940) started out on a pro-Catholic note. With a Catholic majority in the Assembly and the feeling that France's defeat was due to national infidelity, the government decided to build what is now one of Paris's most renowned, if architecturally oddball, churches: Sacré-Cœur, right at the summit of the steep hill of Montmartre—a neighborhood that would have been described as "bohemian" at the time. But the Catholic majority in the Assembly thinned out in subsequent elections; Sacré-Cœur only barely got built, and new restrictions were placed on Catholic teachers and religious orders.

In theory, the Church still held out for governments that recognized the Catholic Church as the one true Church and extended her certain privileges. Leo was neither radical nor aggressive: history had handed him the reality of many Catholic states, and formerly Catholic states, where the government was getting high handed with the Church. But since Catholic states were becoming rarer, many questioned whether Catholics should participate in the politics of governments that don't meet the test of acknowledging and (to some extent) privileging the Church. For Pius IX, confronting this issue late in his life in the form of the Kingdom of

Italy that had seized all the Papal States, the answer was no. For Leo with respect to France, Italy, and other nations, it was yes.

Church and State: *Immortale Dei* and *Libertas*

Leo issued two encyclicals that addressed issues of Church and state: *Immortale Dei (On the Christian Constitution of the States)* in 1885 and *Libertas Praestantissimum (On the Nature of Human Liberty)* in 1888.

Immortale Dei makes the familiar distinction between "liberty" (good) and "license" (bad). On its own, this distinction does no analytic work ("license" may only be "liberty" that the speaker doesn't like), but Leo lets history do some of the substantive lifting. He rejects "tenets of unbridled license which, *in the midst of the terrible upheavals of the last century,* were wildly conceived and boldly proclaimed as the principles and foundation of that new conception of law" (para. 23; emphasis added). Writing just short of the centennial of the French Revolution's Reign of Terror, every reader at the time would have known what he meant.

We must read Leo standing in his shoes, not ours. He saw that even before the French Revolution, Austrian emperor Joseph II declared war on the monasteries in the 1760s, and prior to that religious affairs were taken over by "princes" during the Reformation. The destabilizing of a Catholic "establishment of religion" (as we would call it) had been not only the door that opens the way to persecution but also the accelerator that put it in motion.

So the state must favor the Church—unless it shouldn't, for specific reasons. Unregulated traffic in ideas is bad, but so is coercion in religion. And the "will of the people" is something to be wary of, yet citizens (particularly Catholic citizens) usually should and sometimes *must* take part in governance.

In *Libertas*, Pope Leo affirms the reality of human liberty, contrary to any form of determinism, whether religious (e.g., the Jansenist movement in seventeenth-century French Catholicism) or economic (e.g., Marxism). But human liberty, he teaches, is injured by concupiscence, the inclination toward sin that remains even in the baptized. We know the natural law, and want to follow it, but we frequently fail. Grace comes to help us, without extinguishing our freedom.

Several tempting doctrines deny or weaken this teaching. First, "liberalism." We have discussed the shifting meaning of this term and how it often allied itself with outright revolution in the era 1789–1870. Here it seems to mean a combination of religious indifferentism, the kind that in the nineteenth century had a tendency to turn into persecution of the Church. Leo also condemns "rationalism," that is, not the use of reason but the placement of human reasoning power over God.

Leo XIII and the United States

Several passages in *Immortale Dei* and *Libertas* might lead one to expect that Leo would find the United States hopeless and wicked. But he did not. He took note of the growth of the Church there and expected that growth to continue. He did, however, warn against something called "Americanism": basically, the idea that American democratic procedure should prevail inside the Church as well as in the political system, combined with a form of Modernism holding that validation of religious belief comes from the psyche of the believer and not from natural and supernatural reasoning based on reason, first, and then on revelation.

Leo saw that the US constitutional system, though not in all respects consistent with the preferences expressed in *Immortale Dei*, was nonetheless providing good soil for the flourishing of the Church, and that the US would be important to the Church in the twentieth century and beyond. For that purpose, he founded the Catholic University in America: a graduate school of the ecclesiastical sciences at first, later expanding to other fields and adding an undergraduate college. The Catholic University of America was a vote of confidence not only in the US but also in the city of Washington, DC, which in Leo's time was still a sleepy half-town that people dropped in on when they had business with a federal agency, but not *yet* a large intellectual and cultural center.

Leo and St. Thomas Aquinas

By the time Leo XIII was elected to the Chair of Peter, St. Thomas Aquinas had been neglected for some time. The Age of "Enlightenment" started with a wave of "rationalism" (e.g., Descartes), forgetting that Thomas had himself been a paragon of rational method, that is, advancing by careful logical steps from premises to conclusions. The Enlightenment led to a reaction in the form of irrationalism that started with Rousseau (eighteenth century) and reached its most influential form in Leo's own time, with Nietzsche. That span of time—the seventeenth century through the mid-nineteenth century—saw many great examples of new Catholic piety (St. Robert Bellarmine, St. Alphonsus Liguori, many founders of new orders, etc.), but it did not produce a new Thomas Aquinas, nor a revival of interest in the original.

Pope Leo changed that in an early encyclical, *Aeterni Patris (On the Restoration of Christian Philosophy)*, issued in 1879. Leo refrains from mentioning St. Thomas Aquinas until halfway through, after discussing how the Fathers, especially St. Augustine, made use of pre-Christian philosophy—analogous to the Hebrews despoiling the Egyptians—to help in understanding Christianity. But the chief and special glory of Thomas, one that none of the other Catholic Doctors shares, is that the Fathers of Trent made it part of the order of conclave to lay upon the altar, together with sacred scripture and the decrees of the supreme pontiffs, the *Summa* of Thomas Aquinas, from which to seek counsel, reason, and inspiration (para. 22).

As a result of *Aeterni Patris*, the philosophical background of theology was more firmly reestablished. Consequently, both twentieth-century neo-Thomism and rival neo-Thomisms (such as John Paul II's "existential Thomism,"[3] taught at the Catholic University of Lublin, Poland) became possible; the Leonine Commission (for establishing definitive critical editions of St. Thomas's works) was set up and is still in vigorous business; and Thomism became an unavoidable chapter in the history of philosophy even outside the Catholic Church.

Up Close and Personal:

ST. JOSEPHINE BAKHITA

We do not know the name her parents gave her. Kidnapped at the age of seven or eight in Darfur in 1877, the captors who sold her into slavery called her Bakhita (which means *fortunate*). Bakhita was resold numerous times and abused severely. Her body was covered with scars from both beatings and a traditional process of tattooing. Bakhita was bought in Khartoum by the Italian Vice Consul in 1883 and escaped with him to Italy two years later. She was given to the Michieli family to care for their young daughter.

The Michielis sold all their property in Italy and were preparing to move to Africa permanently. Mrs. Michieli traveled to Sudan to help her husband, who had purchased a large hotel there. She left Bakhita and the child in the temporary care of the Canossian Sisters in Venice. There, Bakhita encountered Christianity for the first time.

When Mrs. Michieli returned to move her daughter to Sudan, Bakhita refused to go; a legal battle ensued. In 1889, an Italian court ruled that because the British had convinced Sudan to outlaw slavery before Bakhita's birth and because Italian law did not recognize slavery, Bakhita had not been enslaved legally. She chose to remain with the Canossians. Bakhita was baptized with the names Josephine Margaret Fortunata in 1890 by the Archbishop Giuseppe Sarto, the future Pope Pius X.

Josephine Bakhita entered the Canossian novitiate and took her religious vows in 1896. Sr. Josephine served as a cook, a sacristan, and a portress for forty-two years in Schio, Italy, where she was known as *Sor Moretta* ("little brown sister") or *Madre Moretta* ("brown mother"). The first publication of her story in 1931 made her famous throughout Italy. A student once asked her what she would do if she met her captors. Her reported response was "If I were to meet those who kidnapped me, and even those who tortured me, I would kneel and kiss their hands. For, if these things had not happened, I would not have been a Christian and a religious today." St. Josephine Bakhita died in 1947.

Leo and the "Social Question"

For the late nineteenth-century Church, the potentially ominous phrase "social question" means the relations of capital and labor in the industrial economy, the burdens imposed on workers, and the challenge posed by socialism, which in those days was often violent and serious about taking all property into the hands of the socialist state they would impose.

Leo's 1891 encyclical, *Rerum Novarum* (*Of New Things*), was itself "revolutionary." Though popes before had frequently addressed political topics in a broad sense, none had addressed the specific facts of economic relationships in an industrializing economy. "Social encyclicals" is a term largely invented and applied by historians post hoc. To be sure, Pius XI wrote *Quadragesimo Anno* in conscious commemoration of the fortieth anniversary of *Rerum Novarum*, and since then, popes who issue encyclicals on economic justice in years ending in "1" know they are building on a tradition that has its own flow. But there is no evidence that Leo thought he was creating a new genus of teaching, and he would probably have a few things to say to those who try to sequester these writings from the rest of papal teaching.

Rerum Novarum declares early on that the condition of workers had become "a yoke little better than that of slavery itself" (para. 3).[4] This is in part because "the ancient workingmen's guilds were abolished in the last century, and no other protective organization took their place." While medieval guilds are viewed as a solution to labor problems by those Catholic thinkers called Distributists, Leo did not call for reviving guilds—only lamenting the fact that no (nonsubversive, nonanarchist, nonsocialist) organizations for workers exist in 1891.

In paragraph 20, Leo gets more specific, listing the obligations of employers (those who owned and invested capital):

> "not to look upon their work people as their bondsmen, but to respect in every man his dignity as a person ennobled by Christian character"
>
> "to see that the worker has time for his religious duties" (In a Catholic society, Sundays off, to allow for Mass and suitable consecration of the day. In religiously diverse countries, states do well to see that employer and employees can fairly negotiate for the desired day off.)
>
> to see that the worker "be not exposed to corrupting influences and dangerous occasions; and that he be not led away to neglect his home and family, or to squander his earnings."

With regard to private charity, the rich do not have to give of their own necessity, "nor even to give away what is reasonably required to keep up becomingly his condition in life, 'for no one ought to live other than becomingly'" (para. 22, citing *Summa Theologiae*, IIa–IIae, q. xxxii, art. 6, Respondeo).

And again: "Inequalities of condition" are inevitable.

"Everyone fulfills an important function. Justice, therefore, demands that the interests of the working classes should be carefully watched over by the administration, so that they who contribute so largely to the advantage of the community may themselves share in the benefits which they create—that being housed, clothed, and bodily fit, they may find their life less hard and more endurable. . . . There is no fear that solicitude of this kind will be harmful to any interest; on the contrary, it will be to the advantage of all, for it cannot but be good for the commonwealth to shield from misery those on whom it so largely depends for the things that it need" (para. 34).

The assumption at work here is that "workers" and "the poor" are virtually identical categories, and further, that these working poor are "apt to be in need of public provision at any moment." Though we should take enduring lessons from *Rerum* as the foundational social encyclical, the situation Leo was observing is different from ours.

Pope Leo was not optimistic about strikes. In Leo's time, ideas such as Georges Sorel's theory of the revolutionary "general strike" were bouncing around revolutionary circles, labor violence was not unknown in the US, and overall, Leo had reason to caution against them as tending to violence.

Today, expressing doubts about women in the paid workforce is unacceptable, while to lack fervor in opposition to all child labor is to be a certified monster. While Leo assumes most of the people he calls "workers" are men, he does not categorically condemn workforce participation by either women or children. Instead he asserts rules to take account of the different needs of each of these groups, and of the family:

> In regard to *children*, great care should be taken not to place them in workshops and factories until their bodies and minds are sufficiently developed. For, just as very rough weather destroys the buds of spring, so does too early an experience of life's hard toil blight the young promise of a child's faculties, and render any true education impossible. Women, again, are not suited for certain occupations; a woman is by nature fitted for home-work, and it is that which is best adapted at once to preserve her modesty and to promote the good bringing up of children and the well-being of the family.

Let the outrage fly. But let it be also noted that one cannot simply recruit the corpus of "Catholic social teaching" for the cause of contemporary first-world progressivism. It has something in it to make everyone angry.

Rerum finishes out by endorsing labor unions, not as fomenters of class hatred, but as mutual aid societies; he links them more generally with "associations," which the Church blesses as long as they are not secret or anti-Catholic, and even with religious orders, though without changing the "state of life" of their members.

Spiritual Warfare and the "Rosary Pope"

In October 1884, Pope Leo is reputed to have had a deeply disturbing vision. As the story goes, he had finished offering Mass in his private chapel and suddenly stopped at the foot of the altar and looked up. Leo stood motionlessly and stared for about ten minutes; the color vanished from his face. He went immediately to his office, sat down, and wrote.

While the pope never recorded what he saw in any official way, he composed the Prayer to St. Michael the Archangel in response to it, asking that the "Prince of the heavenly host . . . cast into hell Satan and all the evil spirits who prowl about the world seeking the ruin of souls." In 1886, he promulgated the prayer and decreed that it be added, along with the Salve Regina, to the "Leonine Prayers" after every "low" Mass throughout the universal Church.

Pope Leo XIII has been called the "Rosary pope," and with good reason. Between 1883 and 1898, he published twelve encyclicals and five apostolic letters on the Rosary. In his earlier works, Leo strived to establish the Rosary as a respected public devotion, not merely one suited to illiterate masses. Later writings emphasized the efficacy of the Rosary as a weapon against threats to the faith and a balm in trying times. Pope Leo presented the Rosary not only as a "school of faith" and a "school of charity" but also as a key to influencing the society at large.

While little research has been done on the source of Leo's confidence in the Rosary, it is useful to recall that Bernadette Soubirous's visions of the Blessed Virgin Mary at Lourdes occurred in 1858. By that time, Leo had been a priest for almost twenty years. Interestingly, Bernadette's death at a young age came in 1879, just one year after Leo XIII was elected pope. What we do know is that Leo observed the silver anniversary of Lourdes as a jubilee year, and that a replica of the Lourdes grotto was placed in the Vatican gardens two years before his death.

Across the Threshold

Before he died in 1903, Leo XIII, with his much longer reign than anticipated or even desired by the cardinals who elected him, guided the Church
across the threshold of the twentieth century. Leo was a "progressive"
pope, not in the political sense of the term but in a descriptive one. Leo
revived Thomism to give a stronger philosophical foundation to Catholic theology; he faced the "social question"; in both his diplomacy and
his written teachings Leo cautiously opened the Church to pluralistic
democracy even while reasserting traditional doctrine on Church and
state; and he took a stern first look at Modernism. Leo not only clearly
reiterated the Church's traditional teachings in an age of rapid change but
also prepared the Church to fight through the challenges that lay ahead,
especially the looming crisis of Modernism to which our next pope would
devote much of his time.

YOU BE THE JUDGE:

Doesn't Catholic "social teaching"
amount to an endorsement of socialism?

Leo XIII's encyclical *Rerum Novarum* is the foundational document of what we now call "Catholic social teaching." The answer
to the "yoke little better than slavery" question in Leo's time was
that of the socialists. "But their contentions are so clearly pow-
erless to end the controversy that were they carried into effect
the working man himself would be among the first to suffer.
They are, moreover, emphatically unjust, for they would rob the
lawful possessor, distort the functions of the State, and create
utter confusion in the community."

Several of the early paragraphs of *Rerum* focus on land as
the source of human sustenance. Leo might not have thought

highly of industry's capacity to provide for human needs, making employment in industry a participation in something profitable (for the owners of capital) but not all that important for the overall economy. But the relative importance of the land economy, the industrial economy (still getting started in Leo's time), matters little, because Leo's point is that everyone, emphatically including workers, should *own* something: a piece of arable land, a share in a factory, or just one's own home. Ownership is important, and Leo would have liked to see it more widely distributed. The system of differentiated capital and labor need not be abolished, but the dichotomy of owners and nonowners should be narrowed.

Leo shows familiarity, and some agreement, with Enlightenment philosopher John Locke's theory that man gains the right to own land by "mixing his labor" with it (John Locke, *Second Treatise on Government*, Chapter V5). But Locke's theory of the state depends on individuals in a "state of nature" agreeing to delegate some powers to government. For Leo, not individuals but families are prepolitical. In this Leo sides with Aristotle against the Enlightenment, except that for Aristotle, the family still needed the city to complete it, while for Leo and the Catholic tradition, the family is not just prior in time but actually superior to the state:

> Provided, therefore, the limits which are prescribed by the very purposes for which it [the family] exists be not transgressed, the family has at least equal rights with the State in the choice and pursuit of the things needful to its preservation and its just liberty. We say, "at least equal rights"; for, inasmuch as the domestic household is antecedent, as well in idea as in fact, to the gathering of men into a community, the family must necessarily have rights and duties which are prior to those of the community, and founded more immediately in nature. (para. 13)

Leo is not very specific about what we may be most curious about: What is the morally compelled extent of redistribution? What is the state's role? It is not to bring about a state of perfect happiness, because it cannot, but even more because "inequalities of condition" are inevitable (para. 34) and because "Jesus Christ, when He redeemed us with plentiful redemption, took not away the pains and sorrows which in such large proportion are woven together in the web of our mortal life. He transformed them into motives of virtue and occasions of merit; and no man can hope for eternal reward unless he follow in the blood-stained footprints of his Savior" (para. 21).

Leo's critique of what we know as "welfare" is not a root and branch rejection but a defense of the Church's efforts and a warning against their displacement by the state. So on one hand, "the public administration must duly and solicitously provide for the welfare and the comfort of the working classes; otherwise, that law of justice will be violated which ordains that each man shall have his due" (para. 33).

On the other hand,

> at the present day many there are who, like the heathen of old, seek to blame and condemn the Church for such eminent charity. They would substitute in its stead a system of relief organized by the State. But no human expedients will ever make up for the devotedness and self-sacrifice of Christian charity. Charity, as a virtue, pertains to the Church; for virtue it is not, unless it be drawn from the Most Sacred Heart of Jesus Christ; and whosoever turns his back on the Church cannot be near to Christ. (para. 30)

Chapter 3

A Crisis in Theology

Pope Leo XIII's pontificate had been outward looking, but by 1903, the Church had some internal problems that needed attention. Born Giuseppe Melchiorre Sarto, in northern Italy, Pius X's early life story follows the pattern of the bright but dirt-poor boy whose parish takes up a fund to send him to seminary. By means of a favor from the Patriarch of Venice (a post Sarto himself would later hold), Sarto was granted a free place at the seminary, where he completed four years of high school and then four years of seminary studies. So, thanks to his own diligence as a schoolboy in Riese, to his determination to be a priest despite initial resistance from his father, and finally to his coming to the notice of the Patriarch of Venice as a suitable scholarship candidate, young Sarto received probably as high-quality a humanistic and theological educational as was available in Italy. He was thoroughly prepared to understand the challenges modernity was posing to the Church in his era.

Fr. Sarto was assigned to a parish in Treviso in 1875, five years after the demise of the Papal States and the rise of Italian Kingdom jurisdiction over the whole peninsula, and three years before the death of Bl. Pius IX. Though not a particularly ambitious man, he moved up steadily from curate. Equivalent to our parochial vicar or associate pastor, this position was not funded by the Church under the ill-organized canon law then in force. Because of this, Fr. Sarto had to depend on the charity of his parishioners—a charity he often reciprocated to those in need. In due course he became a pastor, a diocesan official, and then Bishop of Mantua.

In Mantua, Bishop Sarto's leadership centered on educational reform. In the theological disputes of that era and the decades following, he might well have been called an "intellectualist." A movement, later called Modernism,

was growing among theologians, especially in France. It tended to relativ-
ize the Church's dogmatic statements in favor of how people "feel" about
them. Those called "intellectualists" insisted, as does the Church, on a belief
in the power of rationality, ordinarily possessed by human beings as such,
regardless of their inclination (or not) toward book learning.

Many Mantua priests had simply stopped giving homilies. Bishop Sarto
made them start again, and also paid much-needed attention to the seminary.
Located near the episcopal residence, he visited it often. It was slow but fruitful
work, and it gained for Bishop Sarto his second, and more important, episcopal appointment from Leo XIII: to the Patriarchate of Venice. (Three twentieth-century popes had served as Patriarch of Venice;[1] St. Pius X was the first.)

For centuries as an independent, commercial, seafaring republic, Venice had spread Italian culture throughout the world. Yet it was the youngest of Italy's great cities and had not yet existed during Christianity's first
missions throughout the peninsula. Moreover, it had occasionally gone
through periods of ostentatious independence from Rome, and even (rhe-
torically, that is) from Christianity, notably during its seventeenth-century
struggle against Pope Paul V.

One of Venice's treasures—perhaps the most recognizable one apart
from its canals—is the *campanile,* or bell tower, of St. Mark's Cathedral.
Few know, however, that the bell tower of St. Mark's that we see today
is a carefully constructed replica of the original. The original collapsed
completely in 1902. Patriarch Sarto ordered three days of thanksgiving
for the fact that no one was killed (except, they say, the caretaker's cat[2]).
Sarto believed Our Lady had preserved all endangered human lives in this
incident. (The loss of the cat was regrettable, as he probably kept both the
campanile and the cathedral free of rodents. But Italian cities are never
short of stray cats, so new job applicants were probably not hard to find.)
More significant was the dedication ceremony of the new *campanile.* The
press noted it was the first ceremony bringing together Church and state in
Italy since the fall of Papal States in 1870 and the tense standoff ever since.

With Pope Leo XIII in declining health, the press inevitably picked up
on Sarto's *campanile* speech as a papal audition piece. That's very unlikely to

have been his intent, and there is solid evidence of his nonambition for the papacy. He reacted quite negatively when friends wished him victory at the conclave, replying, "Cannot you suggest some worse misfortune for me?"[3]

Yet he would have had to have been living under a rock, which he never did, to be unaware that he was being talked about along this line. The frontrunner, though, was Pope Leo's secretary of state, Cardinal Rampolla. After the third "scrutiny" (the papal conclave term for "ballot"), Cardinal Puzyna, from Kraków, which was then within the Austrian Empire, announced that Emperor Franz Joseph II would exercise the "Habsburg veto" against Rampolla. This was controversial, as it was not clear that historically Catholic monarchies still possessed the veto power they once had.

Both history and hagiography record several newly elected popes being reluctant to accept. There's a reason the room for the vesting of new popes is called "the room of tears." But in the case of Pius X, the stories are startling. Between two scrutinies, after his candidacy had gained momentum, Sarto went missing, and the secretary of the conclave, a fervent young monsignor, was sent to find him. He did so, in a chapel, and asked Sarto whether he really wanted the message taken back to the conclave that Sarto was unwilling to accept election. Sarto said yes, he'd be very glad if the monsignor would report that message but that it was the wrong answer. Sarto returned to the conclave, and the seventh scrutiny gave him more than the required two-thirds supermajority.

Modernism

In his *Catholic Dictionary*, the Servant of God Fr. John Hardon, S.J., gave this definition of Modernism:

> A theory about the origin and nature of Christianity, first developed into a system by George Tyrrell (1861–1909), Lucien Laberthonnière (1860–1932), and Alfred Loisy (1857–1940). According to Modernism, religion is essentially a matter of experience, personal and collective. There is no objective revelation from God

to the human race, on which Christianity is finally based, nor any reasonable grounds for credibility in the Christian faith, based on miracles or the testimony of history. Faith, therefore, is uniquely from within. In fact it is part of human nature, "a kind of motion of the heart," hidden and unconscious. It is, in Modernist terms, a natural instinct belonging to the emotions, a "feeling for the divine" that cannot be expressed in words or doctrinal propositions, an attitude of spirit that all people have naturally but that some are more aware of having. Modernism was condemned by Pope St. Pius X in two formal documents, *Lamentabili* and *Pascendi*, both published in 1907. (Etym. Latin *modernus*, belonging to the present fashion.)

Most give Pius X high marks across a range of issues—daily Communion for all Catholics, First Communion at an early age, the first codification of canon law since the Middle Ages, and curial reform—all achievements that, while totally Catholic, are also in some way acceptable to almost everyone. Only one issue incites some to take a brickbat to Pius: the "witch hunt" that supposedly was the thrust of Pius's moves against Modernism.[4]

But many evade the question of whether Modernism even existed or exists and, if so, what it was or is. The term *witch hunt* gets us nowhere, except as a tag for the user's belief that the thing hunted does not exist, or if it does, is harmless. Still, we can learn most from the writings of the self-named Modernists, especially Fathers Alfred Loisy and George Tyrrell.

Pius X chose not to name names in *Pascendi*. This was a risky strategy, as it exposed him to the charge of straw manning. But the Holy See deals with erring theologians on a case-by-case basis, and with due process. An encyclical condemning a school of thought could not provide that.

Pius X met the Modernists where they placed themselves: as defenders of the Faith, relativizing the historical truth of the Bible to keep it defensible in light of the then-new "high criticism." At first you try to distinguish secondary biblical narratives from those at the core of Christianity (and Judaism before it, in the Old Testament), but this leads only to the expansion of that "secondary" category.

Leo had written,

> Under the specious pretext of depriving the adversaries of the
> revealed word of apparently irrefutable arguments against the
> authenticity and veracity of the Holy Books, some Catholic
> writers have thought it a clever idea to adopt those arguments
> for themselves. By these strange and perilous tactics they have
> worked to make a breach with their own hands in the walls of
> the city they were charged to defend. . . . While encouraging our
> exegetists to keep abreast with the progress of criticism, we have
> firmly maintained the principles which have been sanctioned in
> this matter by the traditional authority of the Fathers and Coun-
> cils, and renewed in our own time by the Council of the Vatican.[5]

Pius X renewed the Church's response to Modernism in a long encyclical in 1907 called *Pascendi Dominici Gregis* (*Feeding the Lord's Sheep:
On the Doctrine of the Modernists*). Published alongside *Pascendi* was a
new syllabus of errors, entitled (so you know where we stand) *Lamentabili*. *Pascendi* is long and complex. Its ratio of exposition to denunciation
is high, and its exposition ventures into philosophy as well as theology,
history, and biblical exegesis. Because of this, it probably does not get read
as often as it should. Furthermore, its length and detail give it an exposure
to the comeback, "You misunderstood what I/we/they said!" But really,
what were Pius's alternatives?

- Leave the Modernists alone to enjoy their prestige and influence.
  Not an option.
- Write a theological doorstopper in which every leading Modernist's work would be critiqued in detail, with pinpoint citations. This
  could have been done—the phalanx of curial and Roman theologians would have been equal to the task—but if few people read
  Pascendi, how many would have read through a thick brick of a
  papal book? Besides, it would only have facilitated reviews claiming
  "that's not what I meant," which would have been taken as discred-
  iting the whole work, to the detriment of papal teaching authority.

- A short, user-friendly encyclical. This would not have covered the waterfront adequately and might have signaled a lack of seriousness.

So really, *Pascendi* could scarcely have been other than it is. For those for whom a digest version is necessary, *Lamentabili* was issued a few months before. When *Pascendi* dropped, it had more or less the desired effect. Whether in delight or in rage, theologians knew it was both serious and authoritative.

In the end, perhaps the fundamental problem with Modernism was (and still is, if it still exists) not that it tends to corrode Catholic belief but that it aims at "saving" Catholicism by "reconciling" it with "the modern" without acknowledging that what is modern is constantly changing. Modernists would defend the Faith by reconciling it with historical criticism and with "science" (how comically nineteenth century to use this word so univocally). But science is always making new discoveries, and historical criticism has made strides Modernist theologians never dreamed of, some of them tending to bolster rather than erode the credibility of scripture.

The Modernists' proposed "saving" of Catholicism from "science" was, at best, a saving of it from science *as understood in roughly the period 1890–1920*, a project doomed, even if we assume it was as well intentioned as advertised—and that assumption is due for some historical criticism.

Up Close and Personal:

ST. THÉRÈSE OF LISIEUX

Countless books have been written about St. Thérèse of Lisieux. For our purposes, it is worth noting just how much influence a life well lived can have, despite its brevity and lack of tangible achievements. Thérèse was not a foundress. She was neither very rich nor very poor. She was not celebrated or well known. She did not settle any longstanding disputes or solve any Church crises. In short, Thérèse did not accomplish any heroic deeds—other than holiness, that is.

What Thérèse of Lisieux did do was demonstrate the possibility of sanctity for the rest of us. If "nothing is small in the eyes of God," then holiness is available to every Christian believer. If "our Lord does not look so much at the greatness of our actions, or even at their difficulty, as at the love with which we do them," then the "little way" is open to everyone, and we can all become saints. That is why the "Little Flower" has inspired millions of Catholics since her death in 1897 and remains the focus of so much popular devotion.

Interestingly, Thérèse's memoir, *The Story of a Soul*, was heavily edited by her sister Pauline and published one year after her death. Although the book's audience was quite limited at first, its impact was significant. By 1902, the work had been translated into Polish, and a Scottish priest wrote a brief hagiography of Thérèse in 1912, two years before her cause for canonization was formally opened. In order to shorten the process, Pope Benedict XV dispensed with the required fifty-year delay between death and beatification. Thérèse was beatified in 1923 and canonized by Pope Pius XI in 1925, a scant twenty-eight years after her death. Evidently, all the stops were pulled out for the event. Pius XI revived the tradition of covering the outside of St. Peter's Basilica with torches and tallow lamps. Elder workmen remembered how to set the lamps as they had been the last time this was done—fifty-five years prior in 1870—and for two weeks, hundreds of men fastened lamps to St. Peter's dome.

Other Initiatives

In a pontificate much shorter than those of his two predecessors (1903–1914), Pius X pursued a handful of agenda items.

The Pius X hymnal testifies to his desire to improve Church music (*motu proprio Tra le sollecitudine*), above all to foster the revival of Gregorian chant. Renaissance polyphony was also encouraged, but "since modern music has risen mainly to serve profane uses, greater care must be taken with regard to it, in order that the musical compositions of modern style which are admitted in the Church may contain nothing profane, be free from reminiscences of motifs adopted in the theaters, and be not fashioned even in their external forms after the manner of profane pieces." History doesn't record what Pius thought of his countrymen's national pastime, opera, but he wanted to restore the distinction between what belongs in church and what belongs in the opera house or the bandshell ("bandas" were also very popular among Italians).

Second, Pius X encouraged young Catholics to receive their First Communions at the "age of discretion," generally around age seven. The Council of Trent had called for this, but numerous factors resulted in widespread delay of the sacrament to the age of twelve, fourteen, and even later. In the decree *Quam Singulari* (1910), Pope Pius reminded the Church of the efficacy of the sacraments, and that while one should receive them worthily, they were to be seen as not rewards but remedies for the human soul. It is because of this that, while the definition and condemnation of Modernism were probably his most significant accomplishment, many people still think of him as the pope of young children at Communion.

Pius made it a priority to produce a codification of canon law, the first since Gratian in the twelfth century. The ultimate outcome of this initiative was successful, but not in Pius's lifetime. The code was finished in 1917, three years after his death, under Benedict XV, and is therefore known as the Pio-Benedictine Code. It was eventually replaced by the revision of canon law that occurred in 1983. He also successfully reorganized the Curia and finally renamed the Inquisition to the much more palatable Holy Office.

YOU BE THE JUDGE:

Isn't the Catholic Church opposed to scientific research and technological advancement?

The Catholic Church is almost always the most prominent "usual suspect" when it comes to accusations of opposing science and technological advancement. While it is true that the Church spoke out against Modernism, it has never opposed modernization.

Perhaps the most convincing evidence of this is the sheer number of devout Catholics who have made significant contributions to science. Many of these were highly educated priests and religious. In the Modern Era, we can mention Augustinian friar Gregor Mendel, who pioneered modern genetics, and Jesuit Fr. Georges LeMaitre, the physicist who first recognized that the universe was expanding. Sister of Charity Mary Kenneth Keller was the first woman to earn a PhD in computer science (University of Wisconsin, 1965).

It is important to recognize, however, that the Church does examine science and technology in terms of morality and the common good. Most scientists ask only *how* to do something not whether it *should* be done, and law and ethics rarely keep up with the pace of discovery and technological advancement. The development of nuclear weapons during World War II is a clear example of this.

That being said, the Catholic Church has a long history of sponsoring scientific research and endeavor. That's why it came as no surprise when Pope Pius XI founded the Pontifical Academy of the Sciences in 1936 for the purpose of promoting research and development in mathematical, physical, and natural sciences. Membership in the Pontifical Academy does not depend on religious, national, or political affiliation; hence, many Nobel laureates are counted among its members. The Pontifical Academy continues to be a source of objective scientific information, not only for the Vatican, but also for the international scientific community.

Chapter 4

The War to End All Wars

As the struggle for influence and power intensified in Europe, efforts to both prepare for and avoid war also mounted. Pius X had read the writing on the wall by 1912 and even warned his secretary of state that a "Great War" was on the horizon. He was remembered to have said, "I pity my successor," at the Lourdes Grotto in the Vatican Gardens.

In July 1914, Pius wrote a letter to Austro-Hungarian emperor Franz-Joseph asking him to find a peaceful resolution to the Serbian crisis that had erupted, resulting in the assassination of Archduke Ferdinand. The emperor replied with a request for a papal blessing of the empire's arms. Pius refused, saying, "I do not bless arms, but peace." Peace, however, did not come, and Pius X died as the "guns of August" blazed in 1914.

On September 3, Giacomo della Chiesa, raised to the College of Cardinals at a consistory only four months before, left the conclave as Pope Benedict XV. Pope Benedict XV (reigned 1914–1922) is considered by some to have been an unlikely candidate. As a protégé of Cardinal Rampolla, who "lost" the 1903 conclave to Cardinal Sarto (Piux X), Cardinal Giacomo della Chiesa ("James of the Church," if you like translating names) seemed to be on the outs with the dominant "faction" (the Church has factions? Surely not!) in Rome.

But we don't have to relitigate the 1903 conclave (with its "Habsburg veto" against Rampolla). We might examine the question of whether Pius X's appointment of Archbishop della Chiesa as Archbishop of Bologna was a banishment or a boost. Most observers think it was banishment, since it removed him from a high position at the Secretariat of State and kept him away from Rome for most of the intrigue and plotting season. But others point out that it gave him pastoral experience that was very valuable and that he took very seriously. As archbishop, della Chiesa made numerous grueling visits to a geographically large archdiocese that was slipping away from the Faith under pressure from Socialists organizing in both city and countryside. What we do know is that Pius X and Archbishop della Chiesa never really worked together and that Pius X delayed sending della Chiesa the red hat that usually accompanies an appointment to Bologna for seven years. Pius eventually did, however—in the last month of his life.

As an aside, we could note that in the Great Roman Nose-Off, Benedict XV is a very strong contender. Cardinal St. John Henry Newman and Ven. Pope Pius XII had Roman *probosci* of senatorial proportions, but Benedict XV's overall slightness of frame made his beak something special!

Pius X's elevation of della Chiesa to the College of Cardinals put the Bologna Archbishop into the 1914 conclave and among the possible candidates for election. What made him stand out was that he was an accomplished diplomat. The time of the conclave was early September 2014, and the Great War, later called World War I, had broken out barely a month earlier.

The efforts of the weakening Pius X to intervene with the Great Powers to prevent war had been to little avail. Much of Europe was primed for war, and the Allies were no better in this regard than the Central Powers. A German cardinal at the conclave said to a Belgian colleague, "I hope we will not speak of war," and got the answer, "I hope we will not speak of peace." Such were the times—and if the Holy See was to affect anything for the good, it needed a diplomat at the top.

Fortunately, Cardinal della Chiesa was an alumnus of the Holy See's school for its diplomats, then called the Academy of Noble Ecclesiastics. He had served as a high-ranking aide to Cardinal Rampolla when the latter was nuncio to Spain. Later, when Rampolla became Pope Leo XIII's last secretary of state, della Chiesa took the key job of *sostituto*, literally "substitute," but in substance more like deputy.

If popes can be divided into "bureaucrats" and "prophets," Pius X had definitely been a prophet, so a bureaucratic *papabile* had an inside track, especially given his diplomatic gifts and credentials. As a protégé of Rampolla, he was congenial to the French cardinals, yet his affection for the Austro-Hungarian Empire was well known, so he garnered a lot of votes from cardinals in that area, still sprawling at that time.

Waging Peace

Not surprisingly, Benedict's first statement as pope was a declaration of grief and horror at what he called the "monstrous spectacle of this war with its streams of Christian blood."[1] In it, he also stated his official position: "The pope is not neutral," Benedict declared; "he is impartial." To Benedict XV, however, impartiality did not mean remaining uninvolved.

Benedict had a great affection for the Austro-Hungarian Empire as a bulwark of Catholicism in central and eastern Europe. Other than that, he had no biases toward either side of the war. At various times the French press called him "*le pape boche*" (the slang for "German pope"), and the German press called him "*der französische Papst*" or, "the French pope,"—indications that overall he was getting the balance right and being authentically "impartial."

Each side ginned up atrocity stories about the other; their truth value is impossible to determine even now and was quite difficult for the Vatican to determine during World War I, especially without having the resources of a war crimes tribunal. Yet the very fact that each side wanted the Holy See to believe its stories showed that, despite great disadvantages since 1870, the Church's prestige as a moral arbiter was still respected, and even sought. Also, each side had Catholic citizens and soldiers, and therefore an interest in telling them that somehow the pope was on their side.

Besides public and private appeals for peace, Benedict XV began the Holy See's wartime humanitarian work with a decree at Christmastime 1914. In it, he initiated a program of spiritual and material assistance to prisoners of war, thus entering into friendly competition with the International Red Cross. The Holy See's emphasis on prisoners developed into a specialization in reuniting refugees with their loved ones (a specialty that she continued to carry out during and after World War II).

During World War I, papal nuncios in Brussels, Munich, and Vienna (that's one Allied power and two Central ones) visited POW camps to report on conditions. One war crime story that proved to be true was that Germany had deported Belgian civilians. This practice stopped after a plea from Benedict and the nuncio in Munich.

Benedict had many misgivings about Constantinople—capital of the Eastern Orthodox Churches and of the (Muslim) Ottoman Empire—falling into Russia's hands. Nonetheless, through his nuncio, he made formal protests against the Ottoman government's treatment of Armenians, who were mostly Christians and seen as disloyal by the Ottoman state. Deportations, mass murders, and orchestrated starvation by the Turks in this period are what we now refer to as the Armenian Genocide.

In addition to the inherent weakness of a pope appealing for peace when there were nationalistic Catholics on both sides, Benedict's position became even more tenuous when Italy entered the war on May 24, 1915. At first, Italy saw no advantage for itself in entering the war on either side. But diplomats had been pressing the Austrian government for the return of Italian-speaking lands on the Adriatic. Austria refused on two grounds. First, because these were important sea outlets, but perhaps more importantly because admitting the principal of nationality-based sovereignty would have meant the dismantling of the polyglot, multinational Habsburg Empire. Italy's leverage here with Austria-Hungary was basically this: if you don't return our Adriatic ports, we'll enter the war on the Allies' side. When this did not work, the Italian government felt forced to make good on the threat.

This greatly increased the Vatican's difficulties, because from a legal point of view the Church was still a guest on Italian soil. It had lost territorial sovereignty in 1870 and would not get any back until 1929. The German and Austrian embassies to the Holy See were forced to withdraw to Switzerland because Italy demanded that the Holy See be responsible for their "good behavior" if they remained on Italian soil. This would have meant monitoring—and possibly reporting—every cable coming out of any of these embassies, and the Holy See clearly could not do that.

"Nations Do Not Die"

In 1915, Pope Benedict relayed an offer from Germany for a separate peace with Belgium and France. Those countries' resident cardinals were asked to convey this offer to their governments. They refused. Perhaps in reaction, Benedict and his secretary of state, Cardinal Gasparri, issued an apostolic exhortation entitled *To the Belligerent Peoples and Their Rulers*. In it, Benedict coined a phrase he would use again in peace negotiations: "Nations do not die." The belligerents thought the survival of their nations was at stake in the war, and in fact, though nations perhaps do not die, empires do: the German, Austrian, and Ottoman Empires all eventually became casualties of World War I, though Germany, Austria, Hungary, and Turkey did not, and Poland, long divided between Austria and Russia, was recalled to life. The Russian Empire, properly so called, also perished, but the Soviet Union that succeeded it was hardly less imperial.

With "nations do not die," Benedict was trying to show the warring nations that there was less at stake in the war than they thought and that peace offered them a better outcome than clobbering their enemies. None of the belligerents wanted to hear this.

The peace proposal of 1915 became the model for Benedict's Peace Note of August 1917. Incalculable suffering had befallen the soldiers of both sides in the trenches in the meantime, with no significant change in the military situation. But Austria-Hungary had a new (and, as it turned out, its last) emperor: Karl I, now Blessed Karl, beatified in 2004. Benedict consulted with Karl on the Peace Note. The pope could not have found a better colleague, but Karl, in fulfilling the legitimate secular duties of his office, included elements in the note that were anathema to the Allies. Among these were renunciation of reparations and blame for "war guilt."

> With regard to the damage and costs of war, we do not see any other path than that of the general rule of an entire and mutual

remission, justified, for that matter, by the immense benefits of disarmament; and this is even more the case because one cannot understand the continuance of so much slaughter solely for reasons of an economic character.

The note also called for the return of conquered territories to parties on both sides:

But these peaceful agreements, with the immense advantages that flow from them, are not possible without the mutual return of territories which are presently occupied. Therefore, with regard to Germany, there should be a total evacuation both of Belgium, with the guarantee of her full political, military and economic independence in relation to any power, and also of French territory; from the party on the other side there should be equal return of the German colonies.

The Allied powers, of course, wouldn't hear of this: as they saw it, they had greatly diminished Germany and Austria-Hungary, and they weren't going to allow that achievement to be reversed.

In the end, Pope Benedict was not successful in limiting or shortening the war. But his efforts were not fruitless. They established practice and precedents for the Holy See, making overtures for peace through channels that were sometimes public and at other times secret. Even more importantly, they established a Vatican parallel to the International Red Cross for the aid of POWs and refugees, valuably supplementing what the IRC and other organizations could do.

After the Carnage

In addition to his work for peace and relief of prisoners and refugees, Benedict also canonized an interesting set of saints, including Joan of Arc (seen as part of a reconciliation with France), and the seventeenth-century Irish martyr Oliver Plunkett. He declared Ephrem the Syrian, a fourth-century theologian, a Doctor of the Church, thus showing his high regard for the Eastern contribution to Catholicism. Finally, in his 1921 encyclical *In Praeclara Summorum*, he honored Dante, "the divine poet," as "highest" among "the many celebrated geniuses of whom the Catholic faith can boast who have left undying fruits in literature and art."

Italy—still run predominantly by men not well-disposed toward the Church—was apprehensive of the Vatican's new international role. Obviously benevolent even where less than successful, Church leadership would strengthen the Vatican's role in any future negotiations over "the Roman Question," that is, the Holy See's need and just claim for some sort of sovereign territory. Benedict XV did not live to see it. Always on the frail side, he caught pneumonia while waiting for his ride home from a parish visit in a January storm. He died just a few days later, in January 1922.

Up Close and Personal:

THE MESSAGE OF FATIMA

Nineteenth-century Catholic devotion was bolstered by eight Vatican-approved Marian apparitions, including St. Catherine Laboure's Miraculous Medal (1830), Our Lady of LaSalette (1846), St. Bernadette Soubirous and Our Lady of Lourdes (1858), Help of Christians in Bohemia (1866), Our Lady of Knock in Ireland (1879), and an even longer list of claims. In the twentieth century, only four claimed apparitions were approved. Chief among them are the events that occurred in Fatima, Portugal, from May to October 1917.

Three shepherd children, Lucia Dos Santos (age ten), and her cousins Francisco (nine) and Jacinta (seven) Marto, had encounters with the Blessed Virgin Mary on the thirteenth day of each month. The character of the apparitions was prophetic, even apocalyptic. In the thick of World War I, the children were given three secrets. The first was a terrifying vision of hell and encouragement to pray the Rosary daily and make small sacri-fices for the conversion of sinners.

With the second secret, the Virgin asked that the Church establish a devotion to her Immaculate Heart and consecrate Russia to her. Otherwise, she warned, Russia, which was then in the throes of its 1917 communist revolution, would spread its errors throughout the world. The children were told that the war would end, but if Russia did not convert, another even greater war would follow. She promised to send a warning: a great light in the sky. Such a sign did appear in 1938, when the Northern Lights were visible as far south as North Africa. One month later, Hitler invaded Austria.

The third secret of Fatima was a vision of the pope being shot to death and the persecution of the Church; its text was not published until 2000. The secrets were not revealed publicly by the children but were given to the local bishop. It is rumored that they were shared with each new pope upon his election.

By the date of the final apparition, October 13, 1917, thou-sands of people—both believers and skeptics—were coming to Fatima. Tens of thousands, including reporters from atheistic Lisbon newspapers, witnessed the sun spinning violently in the sky, threatening to crash to the earth. Some were so terrified that they cried out. News of the startling "miracle of the sun" was reported worldwide.

The two youngest visionaries died during an influenza epi-demic within three years of the apparitions. Lucia was sent to school and joined the Dorothean sisters but later became a Dis-calced Carmelite. Numerous controversies concerning the reve-lation of the third secret and the proper way to consecrate Russia to the Immaculate Heart arose over successive decades. Pope John Paul II was shot in St. Peter's Square on May 13, 1981—the Feast of Our Lady of Fatima. It is generally accepted that he was the pope of the third secret and that the worst had been pre-vented by the prayers of the Virgin Mary.

While alleged apparitions are thoroughly investigated by the Church, even when approved, belief in such events is not required. Sr. Lucia lived well into her nineties. She died in 2005, five years after her cousins, Francisco and Jacinta, were beatified. They were canonized in 2017, the youngest saints in Church history.

Chapter 5

Totalitarianism

There seems to be no verification for a story that Achille Ratti was actually the first Italian (clerical or lay, pro or amateur) to climb the south face of Mont Blanc,[1] but he certainly loved climbing the Italian Alps. This is not something you would have guessed from seeing him at the job that occupied most of his time before becoming Archbishop of Milan and then Pope Pius XI: librarian, first at the Ambrosian Library in Milan and then at the Vatican.

You also may not have guessed that Ratti had been a papal diplomat who wrote a study of Polish history and had been dispatched to free and independent Poland after World War I to reorganize the Polish hierarchy. There was nothing about him that would have made you think he was one of the few who did not abandon Warsaw when the Soviets marched westward in 1920 against Polish forces that were outnumbered but stopped the Communists anyway. No, Ratti was just a bespectacled little man with a bland, caricature-defying face—but also a man of daring, wisely chosen over higher-profile and better-known personalities.

The Conclave

The conclave of 1922 took five days and went to fourteen scrutinies—rather longer than usual. Pope Pius XI stepped out on the outward-facing loggia balcony of St. Peter's to give the *Urbi et Orbi* ("to the city and to the world") blessing. We think of this as standard practice, but because of post-1870 tensions with Italy, Leo, Pius X, and Benedict had not done it, so it had not occurred since the election of Pius IX in 1846. This fact made it into the multilevel headline that was and still is the publishing signature of the *New York Times*:[2]

CARDINAL RATTI NEW POPE AS PIUS XI,
SHOWS AMITY TO ITALY;
KEEPS GASPARRI;
O'CONNELL AN HOUR TOO LATE TO VOTE;
WILL BE CROWNED SUNDAY
Pope Insists on Blessing Crowd From an Outside Balcony.
REPROVES 'IRRECONCILABLES': 'I Am the Supreme Pontiff
    Now,' He Replies to Their Protests.
WORLD PEACE HIS POLICY
PIUS XI. DIPLOMAT, SCHOLAR, AND ALPINE CLIMBER—
    SAID TO HAVE RECEIVED THIRTY-EIGHT VOTES.

"Keeps Gasparri" refers to his announced intention, contrary to standard practice, to reappoint his predecessor's secretary of state, and he did, right up to the latter's death in 1930 (whereupon the job went to one of the Vatican's best rising diplomats, Cardinal Pacelli, the future Pius XII).

"Shows amity to Italy," "reproves Irreconcilables," and "I am Supreme Pontiff Now," refer to rumors that his decision to give his first blessing from the outward, plaza-facing balcony was made over the objections of cardinals who were "irreconcilable" with Italy. The rumors (or leaks) had it that the "Irreconcilables" tried to badger him out of doing it, making it necessary for him to remind them that he had just been elected to make decisions like that.[3]

The mention of O'Connell being late refers to the fact that Boston's Cardinal William O'Connell had not arrived in time for the voting, due to the slowness of ship travel (likewise Cardinal Dougherty of Philadelphia).

Weimar and Bolshevism

Pius XI immediately began seeking to work with the European powers for peace and welfare. They held a meeting in Genoa in 1922; through various channels, Pius sent messages to this assembly urging freedom for all religions. He also advocated a walkback of German war reparations levied at the Treaty of Versailles. These were a significant cause of Germany's hyperinflation[4]—the kind where you take your wages in cash and then dash to the food store before your money loses most of its purchasing power. An economy like that wipes out the middle class.

Pius also sent emissaries on a dangerous mission into Soviet Russia.[5] This revolutionary state had consolidated its power by 1920 and then sought to take Western Europe, until its armies were stopped in Poland. Pius's envoys tried to secure release of Roman Catholic and Russian Orthodox priests and find ways to funnel papally funded food donations to the Russian people. But the Soviets were only using the prospect of a forthcoming agreement with the Holy See as a way of coaxing other nations into recognizing their revolutionary, tyrannical, and aggressive state.

Destructive New Ideologies

Pius's reign happened to begin the same year in which Mussolini seized power in Italy. Governments throughout history had sought to make cults out of their rulers and themselves—that's nothing new. Street violence and secret police were nothing new. And as for nationalism, it was anything but new to Italians—least of all to clergymen, to whom, as we have seen in the story of Italian unification, it had generally been hostile. But before Fascism, no government or theory of government had openly declared nationalism, leader worship, and the suppression of opposition to be the foundations of a new order that would replace the democratic one. None had declared political freedom and individualism to be (as we might say today) "so last century," while the new era belonged to the state.[6]

The Church had faced violent competition from the state many times in her history, but this had the potential to be the worst. Yet at the same time, Soviet communism—another form of totalitarianism—was consolidating and using its power, with even more open hostility to religion. The Russian Orthodox majority and the Roman Catholic minority were both under persecution in Russia.

Thus, in the postwar chaos, the Church was facing a set of new enemies that must have been bewildering at the time. Italian Fascism wanted no serious competitors to the state. Yet it was nominally anti-Communist, and the Communists were, at the time, even worse persecutors. Meanwhile, a strange new form of totalitarian ideology was taking shape in Germany. A fringe party at first, dismissed by some but known to the Vatican, National Socialism was a threat on the horizon.

"Nazism" was as anti-Communist as its Italian counterpart, but while Mussolini looked to the widely acknowledged greatness of ancient Rome as his inspiration, Hitler and his cronies looked to vague but menacing symbols of a mythical Germanic past. One can perhaps deal with appeals to the Gracchus brothers or Augustus Caesar or even the proto-totalitarian Emperor Diocletian; they are historical figures. But how do members of a modern society deal with appeals to Odin, Thor, and so forth?

Besides this taste for the darker side of German culture—and with all due respect for the complexities of the question whether aspects of Friedrich Nietzsche's philosophy presage Nazism—Pius XI's leading biographer Zsolt Aradi considers it significant that "as a librarian in Milan he had read Nietzsche and other philosophers who glorified instinct and irrationalism,"[7] and therefore had a description of the suspect ready at hand when Nazism came along.

Pius was not taken in by forms of quasi-fascism that claimed to take up the cause of the Church. In Spain, he knew, the chasm between the hierarchy and the working classes had grown dangerously wide by the 1920s, and many who thought they were good Catholics treated the Church as a political party. When persecution of the Church broke out there in the 1930s, Pius must have been grieved but not surprised. As for France, Pius saw the traditionalist *Action Française* newspaper and movement attempt to use the Church for politics—and banned Catholics from participating. Pius had canonized many martyrs of the French Revolution, but he did not want their witness to lead French Catholics toward a movement that merely used Catholicism as a come-on for an ideology of "integral nationalism" and worship of the state.

The Pacts of 1929: Treaty, Concordat, and the Vatican City-State

Solving the Roman Question required taking the temperature of the new Fascist regime on the issue of Catholics and the Church, and this in turn required sorting out some rather extreme opposites. Sometimes Fascist street fighters would destroy Catholic Action offices and damage churches;[8] at other times Mussolini, who was canny enough to know that he couldn't control Italy in those days if the nation's Catholics were against him, made smooth public statements about the Church's role in Italy.[9]

Negotiations between 1922 and 1929 produced the Lateran Treaty of 1929 and its accompanying concordat. The Holy See got almost everything it wanted, especially a sovereign Vatican City, with all the appurtenances of sovereignty (passports, right to send and receive ambassadors, a postal system, etc.), along with Italy's agreement to respect and enforce that sovereignty.

The Roman Question had been answered, and a new papal state—smaller and capable of defending itself only by treaty—was born. If Italy violated the Vatican's sovereignty, only intervention by another nation could remedy that. But as we saw in the chapter on Pius IX, that was true in the old days too: be it Austria or France, the old Papal States often needed foreign assistance to pull their chestnuts out of the fire. One could argue, therefore, that a "mini" Papal State was (and is) just as good as a big one. The existence and international recognition of either one vindicates the principle that the papacy requires some sovereign space to fulfill its universal mission. There's some irony in the fact that the extent of the pope's sovereign space was pretty much the same as what Italy had offered in the Law of Guarantees of 1871. But that would have been a gift from Italy; the Lateran Treaty was an international agreement between sovereigns.

Do the treaty and the concordat mean that Pius XI reached an "agreement with Mussolini"? At some level, yes, because a country under a dictator does not enter into treaties of which the dictator does not approve. At the same time, Mussolini very much wanted an agreement that would satisfy the Church because, dictatorial state or no, he was concerned that Italians should not perceive a conflict of loyalties between the Church and himself. The Kingdom of Italy had suffered under such a conflict in the decades before Mussolini, and that may have been a source of its political weakness—a weakness that Mussolini exploited to take power. Another man could, theoretically, do the same.

For whatever symbolism may be worth, the sovereigns who reached agreement in the *formal* sense via the treaty and the concordat were not Pius and Mussolini but Pius and the king of Italy, Victor Emmanuel III. It's easy to forget that there was still a king, from the House of Savoy, nominally atop Italian government all through Mussolini's years. Mussolini had seized all the real power, but he never dislodged the monarchy and was in theory acting as the king's prime minister. So when the 1929 agreements were signed, they were signed by each side's second-in-command or chief deputy: Cardinal Gasparri, secretary of state for the pope, and Mussolini, "prime minister and head of government," for the king.[10]

The treaty and concordat, by solving the Roman Question, induced some public euphoria about Mussolini among Churchmen, leading to the oft-repeated but ill-supported claim that Pius himself called Mussolini "the man whom Providence has sent us." It could easily have looked that way in 1929. But euphoria ebbs, by definition, and good Church/regime relations ceased to be the case after the regime began violating portions of the pacts, to which we turn now.

Pius XI versus the Fascist Regimes

Encyclicals by themselves don't stop thugs, but Pius could not do other than teach. Pius XI's very first encyclical, *Divini Illius Magistri* (*On the Education of Children*), laid out a schema in which there are "three necessary societies"; that is, whatever else you do or don't join, there are three organized entities that are necessary for maximum human flourishing:

the family or home, civil society (which, it would seem, includes politics but is not limited to it or constrained by it), and the Church. If any of these three expand to crowd out the others, that is an imbalance—possibly even an injustice—and a barrier to human flourishing.

This yardstick proved valuable. In the two years following the concordat, there was a wave of government-directed violence against Catholic Action (a lay association formed to act in conjunction with the hierarchy and very dear to Pius XI) as well as numerous convents and Catholic schools.[11] The pope's response was another encyclical, *Non Abbiamo Bisogno*.

After nine paragraphs thanking the bishops and the members of Catholic Action, he recites the regime's offenses. The young men and women of Catholic Action were first made to sound like criminals in the press; then their organization was disbanded and suppressed. This was enforced by officers visibly chagrined at having to carry out such orders, as well as by toughs in Fascist uniforms who enjoyed it and in whose presence the regular police stood down. These carried out their orders beyond Catholic Action and extended them to the meeting places of small Catholic pious associations.

In short, the polity—or rather one easily separable part of it: the party activists in whom ideological activity and the authorized use of force had been combined—was descending on groups that were extensions of the household and of the Church. In other words, the problem was one not of isolated abuses but of the regime:

> The resolve (already in great measure actually put into effect) to monopolize completely the young, from their tenderest years up to manhood and womanhood, for the exclusive advantage of a party and of a regime based on an ideology which clearly resolves itself into a true, a real pagan worship of the State—the "Statolatry" which is no less in contrast with the natural rights of the family than it is in contradiction with the supernatural rights of the Church. (*Non Abbiamo Bisogno*, 44)

Six years later, aware that monstrous governments were growing, not shrinking, in number and power, Pius XI produced several encyclicals dealing with different threats in different countries: Nazism in Germany, Communism in Russia, the deteriorating Fascist regime in Italy, and new and revolutionary regimes in Mexico and Spain.

Mit Brennender Sorge
(With Burning Concern)

Given the perennial chicken run over what the pope(s) did or did not do to oppose Nazism, *Mit Brennender Sorge*, the only encyclical written in German, takes on particular importance. The encyclical was read in every Catholic parish in Germany on Palm Sunday, 1937; Hitler was furious.

Early on, Pius notes the concordat with Germany that the Church signed in 1934 and its violations by the Third Reich. It is no wonder that rogue regimes like Mussolini's Italy and Hitler's Germany often broke their concordats, typically wasting no time about it,[12] though in the case of the Nazis, the complaints went beyond concordat breaches to the nature of the regime.

Part of the nature of that regime is the official use of the word *God* in the sense that is pantheistic, a result of the Nazis' self-awarded roots in ancient "Germanic" religion. Pius XI observed,

> Whoever identifies, by pantheistic confusion, God and the universe, by either lowering God to the dimensions of the world, or raising the world to the dimensions of God, is not a believer in God. Whoever follows that so-called pre-Christian Germanic conception of substituting a dark and impersonal destiny for the personal God, denies thereby the Wisdom and Providence of God who "Reacheth from end to end mightily, and ordereth all things sweetly (*Wisdom*, viii. 1). . . . Neither is he a believer in God." (7)

Pius then confronts, for the first time in any papal statement, the cult of race.

> Whoever exalts race, or the people, or the State, or a particular form of State, or the depositories of power, or any other fundamental value of the human community—however necessary and honorable be their function in worldly things—whoever raises these notions above their standard value and divinizes them to an idolatrous level, distorts and perverts an order of the world planned and created by God; he is far from the true faith in God and from the concept of life which that faith upholds. (8)

It's out on the table: a state centered on "race" that thereby "divinizes" it and raises it "to an idolatrous level" is "far from the true faith in God." God is universal; theological nationalism is an error:

> None but superficial minds could stumble into concepts of a national God, of a national religion; or attempt to lock within the frontiers of a single people, within the narrow limits of a single race, God, the Creator of the universe, King and Legislator of all nations before whose immensity they are "as a drop of a bucket" (*Isaiah* xI, 15). (11)

Note here the explicit reliance on a Jewish source.

But perhaps the most memorable part of *Brennender* is the exhortation to parents facing heavy pressure to enroll their children in Nazi schools.

> We address Our special greetings to the Catholic parents. Their rights and duties as educators, conferred on them by God, are at present the stake of a campaign pregnant with consequences. The Church cannot wait to deplore the devastation of its altars, the destruction of its temples, if an education, hostile to Christ, is to profane the temple of the child's soul consecrated by baptism, and extinguish the eternal light of the faith in Christ for the sake of counterfeit light alien to the Cross. . . . We know, dear Catholic parents, that your vote was not free, for a free

and secret vote would have meant the triumph of the Catholic schools. . . . Yet do not forget this: none can free you from
the responsibility God has placed on you over your children.
None of your oppressors, who pretend to relieve you of your
duties can answer for you to the eternal Judge, when he will ask:
"Where are those I confided to you?" May every one of you be
able to answer: "Of them whom thou hast given me, I have not
lost any one" (*John* xviii. 9). (39)

Communism and the Common Good

The subtitle of *Divini Redemptoris* is *On Atheistic Communism*, and it is
the atheistic aspect of Communism that was Pius XI's deepest concern.
Both Communism and Christianity tell "stories," as it were, of the fulfill-
ment of history. But for Communism, the narrative is entirely materialistic
and deterministic; the fulfillment-of-history is godless, and Communism
must, and does, reduce the individual to "a mere cog-wheel in the Communist system" (para. 10). Similarly, "[Communism] makes of marriage
and the family a purely artificial and civil institution, the outcome of a
specific economic system. There exists no matrimonial bond of a jurid-
ico-moral nature that is not subject to the whim of the individual or of
the collectivity" (para. 11).

The Church was recovering the idea of the dignity of work in Pius
XI's time. Maybe the Church had never lost it, but if not, some dust had
settled on it and needed to be blown off. Pius reproves those Catholics
in capitalist industrial systems for allowing conditions to develop that
allowed Communism to gain traction with workers and reformers. He
uses the term "social justice" but also defines it: what is essential to the
common good. The phenomenon of liberalism eating its own tail and
turning from small government to a new kind of statism was just getting
into full swing around the time Pius XI was producing his anti-totalitarian encyclicals. But in the case of Communism, Pius saw that rejection of the common good led not to freedom but to its extinction under
a violent state.

Pius makes no apologies for having a "thicker" concept of the common good than do the various forms of liberalism. For example, those who want to reclaim the "Catholic social justice tradition" for today should not forget that one of the most elementary principles of social justice for Pius XI is that

> social justice cannot be said to have been satisfied as long as workingmen are denied a salary that will enable them to secure proper sustenance for themselves and for their families; as long as they are denied the opportunity of acquiring a modest fortune and forestalling the plague of universal pauperism; as long as they cannot make suitable provision through public or private insurance for old age, for periods of illness and unemployment. (para. 52)

Whatever we think of it, we cannot fail to notice that for Pius XI (as for Leo XIII), a basic principle of social justice includes not just the elements of a "safety net" but also a wage that allows working men to support their families. We believe we have attained new heights of justice by aspiring to see that each *individual* is paid adequately as an *individual*. For Pius, a system that pays a man only enough to support himself, so that his wife must also enter the workforce, is *unjust*.

Pius commends "bodies of professional and inter professional organizations" including, but not limited to, labor unions. He urges priests, religious, *and laity* to spread Catholic social teaching, and he warns against Communism's new "Popular Front" political strategy: "Communism is intrinsically wrong, and no one who would save Christian civilization may collaborate with it in any undertaking whatsoever" (para. 58).

Up Close and Personal:

ST. FAUSTINA KOWALSKA AND DIVINE MERCY

Helena Kowalska was born the third of ten children to a poor and devout family in northwest Poland in 1905. She first felt a call to religious life while attending eucharistic adoration at the age of seven. At nineteen, she had a vision of the suffering Christ while attending a dance. She went to the cathedral where Jesus told her to travel to Warsaw and join a convent. She left the next day, without the permission of her parents or contacts in Warsaw, and took with her only the dress she was wearing.

In Warsaw, Helena approached several convents and was refused by all of them. After a few weeks, the Sisters of Our Lady of Mercy accepted her on the condition that she pay for her own religious habit. She worked as a housemaid to earn the money she needed and was permitted to join the order in 1926.

On the night of February 22, 1931, Sr. Faustina saw Jesus wearing a white robe with red and white rays of light radiating from his heart. Jesus instructed Faustina to paint an image of what she saw with the words "Jesus, I trust in you" beneath it. Faustina did not know how to paint. The image that is familiar to us as Divine Mercy was not rendered until 1933, with the help of an artist who was a friend of Sr. Faustina's confessor, Fr. Michael Sopoćko. Sr. Faustina was directed to keep a record of the conversations with Jesus that she was experiencing. She died of tuberculosis in 1938 at the age of thirty-three.

Divine Mercy was exactly what people were looking for after World War I, especially in the shadow of Russia's Communist Revolution and Stalin's manmade famine in Ukraine. The devotion spread quickly. In 1959, however, the diaries of Sr. Faustina and the Divine Mercy devotion as proposed by her were suppressed by the Vatican's Holy Office. The ban, likely due to a review of poor translations, remained in place for nearly two decades. In 1965, however, then Archbishop Karol Wojtyła received permission from the Holy Office to assemble information on Faustina's life and virtues. The ban was rescinded by the renamed Congregation for the Doctrine of the Faith in April 1978, just six months before Wojtyła would be elected Pope John Paul II. Sr. Faustina was beatified by him in 1993 and canonized as the first saint of the third millennium in the year 2000.

Persecution in Mexico and Spain

Few realize the extent to which the twentieth century was (as the twenty-first already is) a time of persecution of Christians and especially Catholics. Our attention is rightly grabbed by the Holocaust, but we need to acknowledge that twentieth-century anti-religious violence did not begin or end with 1941–1945, nor was it limited to Europe, or to Jews, who were persecuted both before and since that period.

In the 1920s, a persecution of the Church erupted in deeply Catholic Mexico. It was answered by a rebellion by Catholic men known as the Cristeros. These were peasants and workers, the very people who, according to the government's ideology, should have been its most enthusiastic allies against the "bourgeois" Church.

Pius XI wrote two encyclicals about Mexico. In *Iniquis Afflictisque*, 1926, he details the two separate waves of anti-Catholic legislation and praises heroic priests. He also singles out for praise the Knights of Columbus, which, though originating in the United States in 1882, had spread to Mexico by 1905.[13] Pius returned to the Mexican persecution with *Acerba Animi* in 1932, after a Vatican-brokered ceasefire between the government and the Cristeros took hold.

In Europe, Spain presented another volatile situation. Since the post-Napoleonic restoration, governments dominated by Liberals had held sway over a zealous but not necessarily learned Catholic population.[14] When the monarchy was overthrown in a referendum in 1931, radical anticlerical forces and tendencies emerged as from the sewers. The worst persecutions began with the far-left coalition government elected in February 1936 and escalated when General Francisco Franco and his colleagues in July 1936 initiated a coup that turned into a three-year civil war. But even from 1931, priests in soutanes were likely to be spat on or beaten up in the streets.[15]

Large-scale killings of priests, monks, and nuns, and burnings of churches, did not begin until 1936. But by 1933 the situation was grave enough that Pius XI issued an encyclical on it, *Dilectissima Nobis*. Against the background of a new, human-rights-oriented constitution adopted after the king's abdication in 1931, the republic had passed a new "Law on religious Confessions and Congregations." Pius jujitsued the Spanish constitution's procedural liberalism against its anti-Catholic intolerance: "We cannot fail to raise Our voice against the laws lately approved, 'Relating to religious Confessions and Congregations,' which constitute a new and graver offense not only to Religion and the Church, but also those declared principles of civil liberty on which the new Spanish regime declares it bases itself" (*DN* 2).

Family: The Ultimate Social Question

Casti Connubii, perhaps Pius XI's most famous encyclical, is about love, marriage, the natural and sacramentalized relationship of man and woman, and of course, most famously, artificial contraception. The long heritage of the Church's teaching on contraception, from imperial Roman times to *Casti Connubii*, is worth stressing. The same held for Protestants, until the 1930s. So, in his day, Pius XI could count on support from many prestigious quarters.

Lambeth 1930

Lambeth Palace is the London residence of the Archbishop of Canterbury. Since the Church of England's separation from Rome in the sixteenth century, it has exercised influence over ecclesial communities throughout the world affiliated with the Church of England, including the Episcopal Church in the United States. Representatives from these ecclesial communities come to Lambeth every ten years for consultative talks. Lambeth 1930 proclaimed many good and holy things, including about marriage. The problem enters with Resolution 15:

> Where there is a *clearly felt* moral obligation to limit or avoid parenthood, the method must be decided on Christian principles. The primary and obvious method is complete abstinence from intercourse (as far as may be necessary) in a life of discipline and self-control lived in the power of the Holy Spirit. Nevertheless in those cases where there is such a *clearly felt* moral obligation to limit or avoid parenthood, and where there is a morally sound reason for avoiding complete abstinence, the Conference agrees that *other methods may be used*, provided that this is done in the light of the same Christian principles. The Conference records its strong condemnation of the use of any methods of conception control from motives of selfishness, luxury, or mere convenience. Voting: For 193; Against 67. (Emphasis added)

The conference did not think of itself as revolutionary—Resolution 16 is a stout one-line rejection of abortion. Yet Resolution 15 was the only one for which vote totals were included in the resolution itself. Apparently someone recognized the significance of this change.

"Clearly felt" was a shibboleth of the era. The American jurist Oliver Wendell Holmes, Jr., for example, held that "the felt necessities of the time"[16] are what should guide judges—"felt" of course by elites among whom Holmes, and the mostly European conference-goers at Lambeth, could be counted. But these "felt necessities" did not guide the pope. (Nor did they guide the *Washington Post*, which opined that "the suggestion that the use of legalized contraceptives would be 'careful and restrained' is preposterous."[17])

The Encyclical

In *Casti Connubii*, Pius restates as authoritative St. Augustine's view of marriage, which was not (despite what is often said) that sex is solely for the begetting of children. In what may have struck older readers in the Holy Office at the time as a rather modern view of marriage, Pius wrote,

> 24. This mutual molding of husband and wife, this determined effort to perfect each other, can in a very real sense, as the Roman Catechism teaches, be said to be the chief reason and purpose of matrimony, provided matrimony be looked at not in the restricted sense as instituted for the proper conception and education of the child, but more widely as the blending of life as a whole and the mutual interchange and sharing thereof.

In summarizing the "modern" view circa 1930, Pius places children first in the rank of victims of what the world considers "evils opposed to each of the benefits of matrimony." The evil in question starts with considering children as a "disagreeable burden." It metastasizes by spreading nonprocreative conduct not only through continence, which is permitted, but also as far as "frustrating the marriage act," which is not. The pope sees no need to be more explicit than that, not after Lambeth. Pius continues,

> Some justify this criminal abuse on the ground that they are weary of children and wish to gratify their desires without their consequent burden. Others say that they cannot on the one hand remain continent nor on the other can they have children because of the difficulties whether on the part of the mother or on the part of family circumstances. (53)

> But no reason, however grave, may be put forward by which
> anything *intrinsically against nature* may become conformable
> to nature and morally good. Since, therefore, the conjugal act is
> destined primarily by nature for the begetting of children, those
> who in exercising it deliberately frustrate its natural power and
> purpose sin against nature and commit a deed which is shame-
> ful and intrinsically vicious. (54, emphasis added)

Pius says "intrinsically against nature," not against an ecclesiastical
law that can be changed, and not against the state's criminal law, though
that was still the case in some places. No, he says, "against nature," not
accidentally or contingently but "intrinsically."

Artificial contraception silences future generations for the present
pleasure of the couple. Even uncontracepted, not every marital act leads
to pregnancy; that's not the standard. The standard is that whatever factor prevents it from doing so must not be something we have interposed
of our own anti-reproductive will.

> Since, therefore, openly departing from the *uninterrupted
> Christian tradition* some recently have judged it possible sol-
> emnly to declare another doctrine regarding this question, the
> Catholic Church, to whom God has entrusted the defense of
> the integrity and purity of morals, standing erect in the midst
> of the moral ruin which surrounds her, in order that she may
> preserve the chastity of the nuptial union from being defiled
> by this foul stain, raises her voice in token of her divine ambas-
> sadorship and through Our mouth proclaims anew: *any use
> whatsoever of matrimony exercised in such a way that the act
> is deliberately frustrated in its natural power to generate life is
> an offense against the law of God and of nature*, and those who
> indulge in such are branded with the guilt of a grave sin. (56,
> emphasis added)

Interestingly, Pius endorses what we now call natural family planning
(NFP), within appropriate and obvious limits:

Nor are those considered as acting against nature who in the married state use their right in the proper manner although on account of natural reasons either of time or of certain defects, new life cannot be brought forth. For in matrimony as well as in the use of the matrimonial rights there are also secondary ends, such as mutual aid, the cultivating of mutual love, and the quieting of concupiscence which husband and wife are not forbidden to consider so long as they are subordinated to the primary end and so long as the intrinsic nature of the act is preserved. (58)

Pius also denounces abortion without ever using that word, calling it instead "the taking of the life of the offspring hidden in the mother's womb." Our current issues were also issues in 1936 (though in this case his reference in probably to the Soviet Union): "There are those, moreover, who ask that the public authorities provide aid for these death-dealing operations, a thing, which, sad to say, everyone knows is of very frequent occurrence in some places." Pius foresaw demand for public funding of abortion and, even if demand for this was "of very frequent occurrence in some places," some in 1930 must have thought him alarmist.

Another War Looms

For a brief period in 1934, the Vatican, Italy, and France entered into a loose anti-German alliance. They had different but harmonious motives: the Vatican and Italy wanted to keep Hitler from intervening in Austria, and France wanted to keep him from intervening in France. At one point Mussolini even sent troops to Austria's border with Germany, in a protective mission. But when Mussolini invaded Ethiopia in 1935, he was isolated by everyone except Hitler, who supplied him with critical war supplies. Mussolini's Ethiopia aggression—provoked by nothing more than defeats there back in the nineteenth century and a fierce desire to conquer *someone*—ended up being everything Hitler could have hoped for to bring Italy into a new war on his side. Pope Pius denounced the

Ethiopian war loudly when it started—but found to his dismay that most Italians (including bishops) were swept up in patriotic fervor. Never mind restraining Mussolini; Pius had his work cut out just to restrain those who supposedly owed him obedience.[18]

After Pius XI's anti-Nazi encyclical *Mit Brennender Sorge* in 1937, conflict increased between the Church and Germany, and relations with Italy became more strained as Mussolini was sucked into Hitler's orbit. In May 1938, Mussolini faced down Church opposition and invited Hitler for a state visit. Rome, capital of world Catholicism, found itself festooned with a very different cross—"one that is not Christ's," Pius proclaimed.[19]

Last Days

Pius XI's last days were largely spent working with Vatican secretary of state Cardinal Eugenio Pacelli to avoid, and then to mitigate, the effects of the new racial and anti-Semitic laws that Mussolini was enacting as his alliance with Hitler strengthened.

Some attention has been paid recently to a purported "lost encyclical" from Pius XI's last years. This was to have been called "Humani Generis Unitas (On the Unity of the Human Race)." Its purpose was to condemn ideologies that proclaim or presuppose racial inequalities as well as race-war theories of history. A draft from Pius's Jesuit ghostwriters apparently reached him in September 1938. It needed his revisions, but he was already declining into his final illness.

The story of "Humani Generis Unitas" has gotten caught up in the axe grinding over the next pope, Pius XII. The text says much in condemnation of maltreatment of Jews, and implies the divine hand in their survival, but follows this up by looking back with approval on the Church's past warnings against the Jews' anti-Christian proclivities.[20] It's a mixed message at best, and the popular expression of our time, "It's complicated," barely suffices. Pius XI's revisions would have led to a smoother text, had he had the time.

Pius XI died on February 10, 1939. With his death, Cardinal Pacelli's role as secretary of state ceased, but his role as "Camerlengo" (chamberlain, administrator of everyday affairs of the Holy See) commenced. He put the draft of "Humani Generis Unitas" in the files, and there it remained until found by journalists after Vatican II and offered to the world complete with suppositious histories about its being "hidden."[21]

Professor John Pollard recites respectfully the case against Pacelli's course of action (filing away, or "hiding," the encyclical) but concludes for numerous reasons "the decision he took was undoubtedly the wisest course."[22]

Much of the text would have angered the Axis; the parts on Jewish-Catholic tensions would have angered the democracies; and on top of all this, Pacelli had no instructions from Pius XI on what to do with the draft. The unfinished document was not all Pius XI left behind. The outbreak of World War II was also left to his successor.

YOU BE THE JUDGE:

Didn't the Catholic Church sign agreements with European dictators?

Some confusion has arisen from the word *concordat*. Some, correctly seeing the word *concord* as the root of the word, infer that a concordat is some sort of description and celebration of concord—that is, harmony, deep-felt agreement—between the Holy See and the other party.

Something closer to the opposite is the case: most concordats are worked out between the Holy See and governments it does not trust; they are arm's-length negotiated agreements between parties who, in most cases, do not particularly like each other. The *Catholic Encyclopedia*, while acknowledging ambiguity in the term, says, "The purpose of a concordat is to terminate, or to avert, dissension between the Church and the civil powers."

Two things to note: One, concordats are therefore most often necessary when "dissension" between the Church and the civil powers is present or anticipated (though they can be used in friendlier circumstances as well). Two, a concordat is about relations between "the Church and the civil powers." A treaty, by contrast, is an agreement between *governments*. One could say, therefore, that the Lateran Treaty is between the Holy See, qua government, and the Kingdom of Italy, while the Concordat of 1929 is between the Church, qua religious body, and that kingdom.

Chapter 6

World War II

The conclave was the shortest in three hundred years. It is said, "He who goes in a pope comes out a cardinal," but February 1939 is the great counterexample. Pacelli had become a close collaborator of Pius XI, especially when the pope was producing his encyclicals against the rising forms of totalitarianism. Popes don't get to nominate their successors, but Pius XI pushed the envelope on that, saying to Cardinal Tardini, the Sostituto at the Secretariat of State, something really subtle like, "Pacelli would make a magnificent pope."[1]

It is sometimes said that Pacelli came from "old Roman nobility," but it would appear that this stems from the fact that several of his forebears were laymen in the papal administrative service. Such families were sometimes called "black nobility" because of the cassocks and soutanes of their employers.

Pacelli was, by most accounts, the right man to lead the Church during yet another world war. Destined for a diplomatic career right from ordination for the Diocese of Rome, Pacelli had been on several important diplomatic errands. He accompanied Archbishop Rafael Merry del Val in representing the Holy See at the funeral of Queen Victoria. Merry, with his English background, was Pope Leo's obvious choice. But Merry's choice of young Pacelli to accompany him is interesting. When Serbia's war against the occupying Turks led to an increase in Catholics present in Orthodox Serbia, Pacelli was again at Merry del Val's side signing a concordat with Serbia. Perhaps it is because Pacelli's doctoral dissertation had been on concordats and on what canon law says you should do when they fail.[2]

Pacelli had also served many years as a senior diplomat in Germany. As nuncio under Benedict XV, he had witnessed Communists seize Bavaria after the fall of the German Empire in 1919. In that uprising, partisans sacked the nuncio's residence and waved revolvers around, an experience that did not convince Pacelli that Communists were peaceable. Recalled to Rome and promoted to secretary of state before the Nazi takeover, he had nonetheless seen the Nazis as a rising extremist party and warned Rome about them.[3]

When Pacelli's election to the Chair of Peter occurred as expected, he took the name Pius as a sign of continuity amid international crisis. There was delight in the governments and newspapers of the democracies. In Germany, however, the *Berliner Morgenpost* huffed, "The election of Pacelli is not favorably accepted in Germany, since he has always been hostile to National Socialism."[4]

Racial Equality

Pius XII chose the Feast of Christ the King as the date for his first encyclical, *Summi Pontificatus*. In it, he doubled down on the theme he had been working on with his predecessor: the equality of the races.

> A marvelous vision, which makes us see the human race in the unity of one common origin in God "one God and Father of all, Who is above all, and through all, and in us all" (Ephesians iv. 6); in the unity of nature which in every man is equally composed of material body and spiritual, immortal soul; in the unity of the immediate end and mission in the world; in the unity of dwelling place, the earth, of whose resources all men can by natural right avail themselves, to sustain and develop life; in the unity of the supernatural end, God Himself, to Whom all should tend; in the unity of means to secure that end. (para. 38)

Later on, he highlights the increasingly multiracial composition of the episcopate and his plans to expand on that trend: "And in order to give external expression to these, Our intentions, We have chosen the forthcoming Feast of Christ the King to raise to the Episcopal dignity at the Tomb of the Apostles twelve representatives of widely different peoples and races" (para. 48).

Apart from Communism, all the totalitarian regimes that were threatening world peace and the Church at the time were racially based. Nazism was of course racist in its very origins. Mussolini's state ideology at first was not, either in theory or practice, but *il duce* had put up no resistance to adopting racism when Hitler isolated him diplomatically. So state-racism (Germany since 1933, and Italy after 1937 or so) and deification of the state (strong in the theory of Nazism and Italian Fascism; equally strong in the practice, even if not the Marxist theory, of Soviet Communism) were the tenets against which diplomatic and humanitarian attention had to be focused.

The Pope Aids the Resistance

When Hitler initiated World War II by invading Poland (together with his then ally Stalin), Vatican secretary of state Maglione got the news very early in the morning and telephoned the papal chamber. After he was told the news, Pius XII went through his morning ablutions, said his Mass, and then started sending instructions to his nuncios. To the one in Warsaw, he sent an order to organize Polish Jews for transfer to the Holy Land. To Bishop Angelo Roncalli in Ankara, Turkey (later Pope John XXIII), he sent an order to gather documents that Jews escaping persecution would need.[5] Besides ordering the rescue of Jews abroad and the sheltering of them in Rome throughout the war, we now also know that Pius took an active part in the internal German resistance to Hitler. To be blunt, Pius XII not only saved the lives of many endangered Jews,[6] but also worked clandestinely and persistently with German officers trying to overthrow, even assassinate, Hitler.

An early dilemma faced by German Resistance, and with which Pius could help, was that the Allies had declared their goal in the "European theater of war" to be Germany's unconditional surrender. This demoralized many Germans who might otherwise have supported regime change in Germany and made them fearful of horrendous treatment by the victorious Allies. It was necessary, therefore, for the Resistance to convince at least one of the Allies that a genuinely anti-Nazi, democracy-friendly Resistance existed in Germany. The United States did not (yet) care, and France was *hors combat* after June 1940, so the Resistors' attention turned to Britain. Churchill, great war leader and anti-totalitarian though he was, was rather dug in on the conviction that there simply was no real internal resistance to Nazism. He needed to be persuaded otherwise.

We've discussed elsewhere the fraught relationship between Protestant England and the papacy. But taking one thing with another, the new Pope Pius XII, with his diplomatic experience and his help with his predecessor's anti-totalitarian efforts, had credibility. If he vouched for the leaders of the German Resistance, Britain might secretly acknowledge them and—crucial point—be willing to treat them publicly as nonenemies following what we have until now delicately called "regime change" but that we might call, with pride as well as candor, blowing up Hitler.

Pius XII agreed to get involved in this effort,[7] although not precipitately; he, like Churchill, needed reassurances that he was dealing with the real thing and not, for example, with Nazi entrapment agents. The key intermediate starting in 1939 was a devout and fearless Catholic Bavarian lawyer named Josef Müller.[8] Using a bogus and dangerously obtained Nazi cover, Müller ran errands between Berlin and Rome—always (because Pius was not ignorant of spy "tradecraft") dropping his Resistance communications off with trusted monsignors and Jesuits who would see that the pope learned their contents and sent a reply.[9]

By mid-1940, the British were persuaded, but when Hitler invaded westward, imposing occupation on Belgium, Holland, and France, he enjoyed his last uptick of popularity in Germany, and the plotters lost their nerve for a time. Nevertheless, Pius kept the door open to the Resistance, with the help of two assistants in particular, Msgr. Ludwig Kaas and Fr.

Robert Leiber, S.J., who acted as his "cut-outs" for communications with the Resistance via Josef Müller.

When Mussolini was ousted in July 1943, it was with a push that Pius had helped prepare. US Vatican representative Myron Taylor was FDR's liaison on coup planning from Pius; Vatican secretary of state Maglione was Pius's for receiving FDR's responses. Reliable Archbishop Montini, from Maglione's staff, met with a Princess of Parma, or at least a lady who claimed to be this, and who was a cutout for the general who would eventually, if he would ever make his move, be the peace-seeking replacement for Mussolini: Marshal Pietro Badoglio. Through his nuncio to Italy, Archbishop Francesco Borgongini Duca, Pius reached out to King Victor Emmanuel III. Everybody at the top had a cutout. It was spy time.

When the coup came it was carried about by the king and the Fascist Grand Council, who informed Mussolini his services were no longer required. He was ushered into a police car and taken up north. (Later, with German support, he restored his rule in a northern region near Lake Garda with violently contested borders and grandly labeled the region "the Italian Social Republic." When the Allies threw the Germans out of northern Italy in April 1945, anti-Fascist bands caught and shot Mussolini, his mistress, and his chief ministers and strung them up upside down.)

Bordering the Reich

At the time of Mussolini's dismissal by the king in July 1943, US and British forces were marching toward Rome from the south. The Germans swooped down on Rome before the Allies got there. Author and espionage journalist Mark Liebling summarized the situation:

> The Holy See now bordered Hitler's Reich. A white line marked
> the frontier between the arms of the Bernini colonnades. On
> one side stood German soldiers in black boots and helmets
> with carbines on their shoulders and Lugers on their hips. On

the other side were the Pope's Swiss Guards, in ruffled tunics
and plumed hearts, holding medieval pikes in white gloves.[10]

Thus began the ten months of greatest personal peril for Pius and the
Vatican during the war. Of course the Germans, while they were there,
made efforts to round up Rome's Jews for deportation and execution. The
Vatican buildings, still housing Allied embassies, had room for only 477,
but 4,238 found safety in Rome's monasteries and convents. The Germans
got 1,007 others, of whom only 15 survived. But 4,715 were saved directly
by the Church.[11]

Up Close and Personal:

ST. MAXIMILIAN KOLBE AND ST. TERESA BENEDICTA OF THE CROSS (EDITH STEIN)

The horrors of the holocaust are difficult to overstate. Six million
Jews and at least six million others were systematically wiped
out by Nazi forces at extermination camps scattered throughout
Central and Eastern Europe.

St. Maximilian Kolbe, a Polish Franciscan priest, was known
for his deep Marian devotion. Kolbe was the publisher of a Polish Catholic magazine, *The Knight of the Immaculata*, with a cir-
culation in excess of one million subscribers. He traveled to the
Far East and established a monastery just outside Nagasaki,
Japan. After Germany invaded Poland, Fr. Kolbe sheltered two
thousand Jewish refugees and continued to publish religious
works—including anti-Nazi material. His monastery was shut
down in February 1941, and he was one of five priests arrested

by the Gestapo. A few months later, Kolbe was transferred to Auschwitz, where he continued his priestly ministry as possible and was subjected to brutal beatings. According to eyewitnesses, Fr. Kolbe volunteered to take the place of another prisoner who was one of ten men selected to die in a starvation bunker. He outlived the other nine and was executed by lethal injection on August 14, 1941, the Vigil of the Assumption of Mary.

St. Teresa Benedicta of the Cross is more commonly known by her birth name, Edith Stein. Born to an observant Jewish family in Germany on the Feast of the Atonement (Yom Kippur) in 1891, Edith was an exceptionally gifted student. By the time she went to university, however, Edith had become an atheist. She studied under some of the greatest philosophic thinkers of her day and had a promising career before her. Things changed, however, in the summer of 1921, when Edith visited the widow of a friend who had died in World War I and happened upon the *Autobiography of Teresa of Avila*. She was captivated by Teresa's words and stayed up all night reading. Edith was baptized a few months later in 1922.

Though her desire was to become a Carmelite, she was told to wait because her conversion had been painful for her family. In the meantime, Stein lectured to women's groups across Europe on the education and role of Catholic women. Many consider her a feminist. When Nazis blocked Jews from teaching, Edith Stein entered the Discalced Carmelite monastery in Cologne, taking the name Teresa Benedicta of the Cross. Because she was born a Jew, she was required to wear the yellow Star of David on her habit. She was eventually moved to the Netherlands to avoid the Nazi threat. Less than one week after the Dutch bishops released a statement condemning Nazi racism in 1942, an order was given to arrest all Jewish converts. Edith Stein and her sister Rosa, who had also become Catholic, were among 987 prisoners transported to Auschwitz on August 7, 1942. They were killed in the gas chambers there.

The Resistance Revived

Sometime in 1943 the German Resistance welcomed to its cause a new hero: Col. Count Claus von Stauffenberg. Badly injured in Tunisia, he had time during convalescence to reflect on the opposition between the ideology of the state he had been fighting for and his Catholic faith. He got in touch with Josef Müller. By this time Müller was in prison, but he managed nonetheless to communicate with Rome about Stauffenberg. (In a twist typical of Müller's career, his Wehrmacht jailer was in the Resistance.)

With Stauffenberg reinvigorating them, Pius promised to help the plotters attain international recognition, and even to meet with them before the plot's accomplishment date of July 20, 1944. If the coup succeeded, Germany would be led by former Leipzig mayor Carl Goerdeler, former Gen. Ludwig Beck (a friend of Pius's from his days as nuncio in Germany[12]), former Ambassador Ulrich von Hassell[13]—and Müller as its ambassador to the Holy See.[14]

The coup did not succeed. Hitler, who had improbably survived several assassination attempts, survived this one too. The meeting at which Stauffenberg's bomb was to go off was transferred (by Hitler) from a bunker where one fist-size unit of plastique would have seen off everyone in the room, to an aboveground venue with windows where much of the force of the explosion would be absorbed by shattering wooden walls; Stauffenberg, due to his injuries, was only able to set the acid-based fuse on one fist of plastique before his Wehrmacht minder told him to get out of the bathroom and come back to the meeting. Back in the room, Hitler moved a few feet away from the briefcase containing the bomb. Stauffenberg and an aide got out of the briefing room, heard the explosion, and flew back to Berlin to give the prearranged orders based on the assumption that Hitler was dead.

While the fate of the world hung in the balance, Stauffenberg's supposed allies hesitated, waiting for confirmation of Hitler's death that never came. The day that could so easily have been Germany's liberation from Nazism ended with Count von Stauffenberg kissing his crucifix and crying

"Long live holy Germany!" as he faced a firing squad arranged by men he had arrested hours earlier. After the failure of the July 20 plot and the sadistic pursuit and execution of its leaders, Pius XII's opportunities for espionage were at an end.

Pius and the Jews in Real Life

As soon as Mussolini entered the war on Hitler's side, on June 10, 1940, Pius held a meeting with Ugo Foa, the president of Rome's Jewish community. Foa brought with him a letter from Nahum Goldmann, president of the World Zionist Organization, thanking him for his "unflinching support of the Jews."[15] At this meeting, Pius promised to have his nuncios intervene with governments taking oppressive measures and to take special care of those in the Roman ghetto by using the Pallottine Fathers' rescue network.[16]

News of the Holocaust seeped out sporadically; the Nazis didn't advertise it. One Fr. Pirro Scavizzi gained an audience with Pius XII on May 12, 1942, to bring him important news personally. Fr. Scavizzi had been traveling on an Italian medical train through Poland and German-occupied Russia, he said, and one by one, German officers took him aside to tell him things that burdened their consciences. They did not expect their stories to be believed, but they had seen multiple thousands of Jews being taken into concentration camps too small to house them all, but never saw any coming out. There was more: a previously obscure place in Poland—Oswiecem, or Auschwitz, was its name—where officers frequently smelled burning flesh. It happened too often to be a fluke, and too many officers noticed it for any of them to have been mistaken. Fr. Scavizzi thought the pope should know what these officers told him and the suspicions it was raising.[17] Pius XII collapsed in tears.[18]

YOU BE THE JUDGE:

Should Pius XII have spoken out explicitly against Nazi treatment of the Jews?

The question must be phrased this way, because if asked the question with less specific phrasing, such as, "Should Pius have denounced Nazi treatment of the Jews?" his answer would have been, "I did. And the Nazis left no doubt they had gotten the message."

His stance would be based on elliptical references that, though unmistakable and in their time unmistaken, stopped short of the words "the Jews" or any other recognized reference to them ("Hebrews," "children of Israel," "God's elect as narrated in our canonical Old Testament," etc.). So the question has to be, "Did Pius XII do wrong in stopping short of such an expression?"

According to his household manager, Sister Pasqualina Lehnert, Pius began composing a "fiery" denunciation that would have been specific and explicit regarding what was being done to the Jews (see Pollard, *The Papacy in the Age of Totalitarianism*, p. 337). Before he could complete it, though, the Dutch bishops released a statement. In response, the Nazi occupiers of the Netherlands *expanded* deportations. One of the victims was Edith Stein, a.k.a. St. Teresa Benedicta of the Cross. No one can tell whether they would have done this anyway. At the time, though, the lesson learned was that the Church was dealing with the kind of beasts who, whatever their intentions in the absence of Church protest, would use Church protests as a pretext to dial up their atrocities. In light of this, Pius XII had to choose between risking the Dutch experience on a wider scale or remaining silent with all sides concluding that he did not care. Instead, he found a middle way.

Historian Robert Graham, S.J., began researching this difficult period in 1963, at the behest of the newly elected Pope Paul VI. (Paul VI, by the way, had personal knowledge of relevant facts which, even twenty years later, he could not speak about as pope.) Fr. Graham found that several Allied and neutral governments went to Pius during autumn 1942 and asked him for an explicit statement, the kind that would *probably* satisfy his critics today.

At one level, Fr. Graham's account is embarrassing for Pius: not only was a specific and explicit statement theoretically possible, but also diplomats with whom Pius was otherwise working closely (and others) were asking for such a statement. But they themselves were not broad-spectrum humanitarians or disinterested advocates for the rights of Jews: they represented the interests of their governments, and those interests lay in winning the war at hand.

Britain's ambassador to the Holy See, Sir Martin D'Arcy, was more sensitive to the moral crisis caused by German atrocities *and* to the pope's position. All summer and fall of 1942 he shared data on German atrocities, vetted by British intelligence, with Pius—and, what a coincidence, that information was then broadcast on Vatican Radio. There's more than one way to "speak out."

Myron Taylor, the American representative, visited Pius with a speak-out-now message in September, while his government was still sitting on the Reigner telegram. The August 8, 1942, message alerted the governments of the United States and Great Britain to the German plan for mass extermination of Jews in Europe. Others who requested a statement from the Vatican were France (meaning Charles de Gaulle's government in exile in London, not an actual power) and Brazil, Freemason-dominated since before independence. So the pope gave a speech at Christmas 1942 that left the Nazis and Allies in no doubt that he was attacking the Nazis' treatment of the Jews—but, critically for later debates, he did not mention this with the degree of specificity demanded by the Allied diplomats—or by the judges of history.

Chapter 7

The Cold War and Age of Benign Liberalism

The guns were silent, the extermination camps were discovered and liberated, but the list of postwar problems was long and growing. Among them were dealing with "displaced persons" (trying to reunite families, as the Vatican had done after World War I); the problems of eastern European Catholics and dioceses in Soviet-controlled areas of Europe; and the possibility that the Iron Curtain, which was not fixed on Victory in Europe Day (VE Day), could still move westward.

Postwar Communism

Like later popes and American statesmen, Pius XII had always been dismayed that the Yalta agreement in February 1945 between FDR, Churchill, and Stalin had in effect ceded control of Eastern Europe to domination by Soviet Communism. As a fig leaf to his allies, Stalin had promised free and democratic elections in those countries where, by means of his troops, he would retain control. Historians debate whether either of the two Western leaders believed this (FDR may have, Churchill probably did not). The war against Hitler, however, was not yet won, and though shameful, the Allies needed the ruthless tactics of the Soviet Army to slice through Poland, reach Berlin, and end the Third Reich.

Being filled with Red Army troops, Poland slid seamlessly from Nazi to Communist totalitarianism. In other countries east of the Oder-Neisse line, the Soviets relied on Bolshevik bureaucratic tactics: whatever the exact means, victory went to those who went to all the meetings and stayed to the end to vote. In Tito's Yugoslavia, voters were offered two parties, but only the Communists actually existed. Even so, the fictional party won 5 percent of the vote, but the Communists took the other 95.[1] In Hungary, the Soviets tried allowing a free vote, but when the Communists lost it decisively, they forced their way into a governing "coalition" with the victorious party, and from there, they worked their way to power with accusations of Nazi collaboration against their rivals and rigged local elections. The Red Army continued doing what it had been doing on its march through Poland; indeed, two Hungarian Catholic bishops were shot when they attempted to defend village girls.[2] By 1949, the country was the Hungarian People's Republic, under the strict Stalinist Mátyás Rákosi.

When Czechoslovakia showed interest in taking part in the Marshall Plan, its foreign minister, Jan Masaryk, was summoned to Moscow and (remarkably, given Stalin's track record) allowed to return. But back in Prague, he "would subsequently be found dead and broken beneath a high window."[3] In Romania, the Communists had fewer than a thousand members, but with those, the Red Army, and the NKVD secret police on the scene, they were able to stage demonstrations that persuaded the Allied command to let a party closely allied with the Communists join the government. It then proceeded to knock off enemies, as in Hungary, and in 1947 they were able to force the king to abdicate and proclaim a People's Republic.

Italy and the "Iron Curtain"

Thus we come to Italy in 1948, and we've seen this movie before. Italy's Communist Party was large, larger than in some of the countries that had already slipped behind the Iron Curtain, or soon would. It had the potential to win a majority, and if it didn't there was also the Socialist Party, which was closely allied with the Communists. Like similar parties in Eastern Europe, it would find a place within a Communist-dominated "coalition" government.

Let's be clear. This was 1948, and Stalin would live until 1954. Until then, *all* Communist parties, including those in Western Europe and the United States, were Stalinist. Even afterward, de-Stalinization did not mean de-Sovietization. Today we are extremely used to European socialist governments where "socialism" means liberal democracy with a capacious welfare state, and usually nothing more: Britain, the Scandinavian countries, France, Germany, Italy, Spain, and Portugal have all had such governments. We need to consider older situations—1930s Spain, for example—and remember that then, "Socialist" had all the revolutionary, Jacobin, and paramilitary connotations it had throughout the nineteenth century.

The Italian Communist Party's likely coalition partners in 1948 were more like that. So a victory for the Communists, or even for a Communist-Socialist coalition, would have meant that the Iron Curtain no longer extended "from Stettin in the Baltic to Trieste in the Adriatic," as Churchill had put it in his 1946 speech at Westminster College in Fulton, Missouri. Such an election result would have moved the southern end of the Iron Curtain into the Tyrrhennian Sea, west of Italy. And Italy could well have become yet another Soviet satellite state, with all the implications imaginable for the Holy See.

Pius XII had never been in greater personal danger, except perhaps when the Nazis rolled into Rome in 1943. By 1948, Communists had suppressed churches and exterminated millions of Christians in territories they controlled for more than thirty years. Cardinal Aloysius Stepinac of Zagreb stood accused by Yugoslavia's new Communist rulers of collaborating with the Independent State of Croatia,[4] and was sentenced to prison.[5] In 1949, after being imprisoned by Hungarian fascists during the war, Cardinal Mindszenty would undergo torture, a show trial, and imprisonment by Hungary's new rulers.[6] There, but for the grace of God went Italy's Christian Democratic Party, anti-Communists all over the world, Pius XII, and the entire Vatican.

The Christian Democrats won, however, bringing to power—and to the task of rebuilding Italy—Mr. Alcide de Gasperi, Italy's first postwar prime minister. He was a Catholic and friends with Pius XII but felt free to disagree with him on intermediate issues. In 1949, well after the big election, Pius excommunicated most Communist Party members. Exceptions were made for those who had joined it under compulsion, and compulsion included fear for one's job. The Communists were furious. In Italy they had been accustomed to making outward shows of Catholic piety, but faced with the defeat their ideology books said was impossible, they needed someone to blame. The easiest scapegoats were those awful *priests* who are always in cahoots with the *landlords* and other *rich*. The excommunication led to more and more candid anticlericalism by the Communists.

Nonetheless, the move has been considered harsh, especially since he had not excommunicated the Nazis. There are a few points to consider. One, when the Nazis were in power, Pius didn't excommunicate Communists either. To have excommunicated the first would have required the same for the second. Two, many if not most Nazis were Lutherans if they had any religious affiliation at all other than Nazi neo-paganism. Third, while Nazism persecuted the Church as a by-product of other policies and beliefs, or as the result of churchmen speaking against them, Communism had the extermination of religion in general as a precept, and especially the elimination of the Catholic Church. (They were also ferocious against the Russian Orthodox Church in particular through the 1930s, but during the war they found they needed it as a source of national unity.) Fourth, though Italy was no longer a "Papal State" in any sense, it nonetheless remained the Vatican's "backyard." This brings us to the fifth point: most Italian Communists still had some tenuous connection to the Catholic Church. Those who renounced it when they became Communists were beyond the reach of excommunication, but for many who had not, excommunication could have the effect it is always meant to have: remedial.

1950: A Banner Year

Nineteen fifty was a year of great significance for the Church and for Pope Pius personally. Declared a Holy Year, many pilgrims came to Rome, and much of a respectful world's attention was focused there. It was the centennial of the restoration of the hierarchy in England and Wales, and Pius made a broadcast to a stadium full of "RCs" there. It was the year in which he raised Maria Goretti to the altars and made her the Church's youngest canonized saint. It was also the first canonization ceremony in history to be attended by the saint's mother. In December, Pius announced that a decade of archaeological research had confirmed that the remains of St. Peter the Apostle had been discovered deep under the main altar of the Basilica.

Above all, 1950 was the year of the proclamation that the Church's ancient belief in the assumption of Mary was a dogma of the Church. This was the occasion for major Roman ceremony and the release of the encyclical *Munificentissimus Deus*. It was the first exercise of the solemn extraordinary magisterium since Vatican I, and the most recent to date.

Up Close and Personal:
ST. JOSEMARÍA ESCRIVÁ

Fr. Josemaría Escrivá was a Spanish priest and the founder of Opus Dei (which means "God's Work"), an organization of laity and priests dedicated to finding sanctification through the responsibilities of daily life. Born in 1902, Josemaría first envisioned Opus Dei as a young priest in 1928; he initiated it in Madrid. With Opus Dei, Fr. Escrivá charted a groundbreaking and unfamiliar path, one that stirred both support and opposition. Through his considerable organizational skills, Fr. Escrivá gave life to countless initiatives in charity and evangelization, fostered vocations to priesthood and religious life, and mobilized vast numbers of lay people in the work of the Church.

Opus Dei was given final pontifical approval by Pope Pius XII in 1950, and by the time of Josemaría's death in 1975, there were more than sixty thousand members of Opus Dei in eighty countries. After Escrivá's death, Pope John Paul II established Opus Dei as a "personal prelature," subject only to its own prelate and the pope. As such, Opus Dei's work is intended to complement that of the dioceses.

St. Josemaría's 2002 canonization was not without controversy. While many have been inspired by his charity and zeal for holiness, others expressed concern about what they saw as an explosive temper and vain ambition. The best answer to such objections may, however, be found in St. Josemaría's own words: "A saint is a sinner that keeps trying."

The Assumption of Mary

What is this teaching? Pius XII explains (para. 4) that it is tightly interwoven with another teaching long confessed by the Church and proclaimed in 1854, that of the Immaculate Conception. If Mary, by a singular privilege, was protected from original sin and its effects via the foreseen and anticipated merits of Christ's passion, then "as a result she was not subject to the law of remaining in the corruption of the grave, and she did not have to wait until the end of time for the redemption of her body" (*Munificentissimus*, para. 5).

The belief of the faithful in the assumption can be traced back at least to the sixth century, when Gregory of Tours, chronicler of the early Franks, mentions it. There are earlier works that purport to describe it, but these writings are considered "pseudepigrapha," that is, their authors used the name of an earlier, more authoritative writer as a pseudonym, and so are considered unreliable. (One fifth-century writer even claimed his work was by St. John the Evangelist!) But even these attest to a widespread belief in the assumption dating back nearly to the age of Augustine. Gaul (later France) seems to have celebrated the assumption before the Church in Rome did, but it was celebrated at Rome under Pope Sergius I (ca. 700). The scholarly Pope Benedict XIV (reigned 1740–1758) raised this teaching to the status of (in the words of the 1911 *Catholic Encyclopedia*) "a probable opinion, which to deny were impious and blasphemous."

Centuries, perhaps more than a millennium, before 1950, the precursor facts to a solemn papal definition of the assumption were well in place. In addition, Pius hoped that in a world recently recovered from one materialist ideology but still threatened by others, Mary's instantiation of doing the will of God might be a good example. In *Munificentissimus Deus*, he expressed this hope:

> And so we may hope that those who meditate upon the glorious example Mary offers us may be more and more convinced of the value of a human life entirely devoted to carrying out the heavenly Father's will and to bringing good to others. Thus, while the illusory teachings of materialism and the corruption of morals that follows from these teachings threaten to extinguish the light of virtue and to ruin the lives of men by exciting discord among them, in this magnificent way all may see clearly to what a lofty goal our bodies and souls are destined. Finally it is our hope that belief in Mary's bodily Assumption into heaven will make our belief in our own resurrection stronger and render it more effective. (para. 42)

So in a culmination of centuries of belief and celebration, Pius held up Mary in a dramatic way in 1950 as the best example we have of doing the will of God. The definitional text of the dogma, at paragraph 44 of *Munificentissimus Deus*, reads,

> By the authority of our Lord Jesus Christ, of the Blessed Apostles Peter and Paul, and by our own authority, we pronounce, declare, and define it to be a divinely revealed dogma: that the

> Immaculate Mother of God, the ever Virgin Mary, having completed the course of her earthly life, was assumed body and soul into heavenly glory.

Did Mary die? Death is a consequence of original sin, so Mary would appear to be exempt from it. Furthermore, physical death is the separation of soul from body (to be reunited eventually). But if Mary was assumed "body and soul" into heaven, it would seem she never had to undergo this. On the other hand, *Munificentissimus* stops short of saying she died. What's more, this writer heard the esteemed Fr. John Hardon, lecturing to a theology class, say that he had seen a draft of *Munificentissimus* in which paragraph 44 read, "The ever Virgin Mary, after her death, was assumed" and so forth. In Pius's handwriting, the words "after her death" had been crossed out, and the words as they stand now—"having completed the course of her earthly life"—were written in.

The Holy Spirit at work. So, we don't know whether Mary died or not. Pius changed the text that affirmed it, and the question remains open. It wasn't part of what the Holy Spirit wanted us to have certainty about, and may never be. She was assumed body and soul into heavenly glory. This we needed to know, in the grim postwar and on the cusp of a more glittering but still grim age of apparent prosperity.

Up Close and Personal:
PADRE PIO

Born in 1887, Francesco Forgione was drawn to prayer from an early age and admitted to the Capuchin novitiate at the age of fifteen. Fr. Pio was ordained to the priesthood at twenty-three, and the Mass remained the center of his spirituality for the rest of his life. Long pauses of silent contemplation were common when Fr. Pio celebrated Mass, and sometimes his liturgies lasted for hours. His reputation for holiness spread far and wide, and many pilgrims sought his counsel, especially in the Sacrament of Reconciliation. Fr. Pio received the stigmata, the crucifixion wounds of Christ, in 1918. He bore these painful wounds patiently for fifty years and endured countless physical and psychological examinations by both medical and Church authorities. Several negative and accusatory evaluations were made.

Initially, the Vatican imposed restrictions on Padre Pio in the 1920s to reduce publicity. Authorities disallowed him to offer Mass in public, give blessings, answer letters, or reveal his stigmata. Nonetheless, stories of miraculous healings, bilocation, the ability to read hearts, prophecy, conversions, and even alleged physical fights with demonic powers continued, and swelled the crowds who came to the small village where he lived.

Popes handled the reports of supernatural occurrences differently. Pius XI lifted the restrictions that had been placed on Pio's ministry. Pius XII encouraged people to visit him. John XXIII was skeptical and suspected fraud. Paul VI dismissed all accusations against him before his death in 1968, and John Paul II beatified and canonized him.

Last Years

In 1953 Pius held a consistory—a ceremony for elevating nominated cardinals—the last of his reign. In his address, he lamented the absence of new Cardinals Stepinac and Mindszenty; both had been imprisoned by their Communist governments. He also mentioned another absent new Cardinal, Stefan Wyszyński, Archbishop of Warsaw. Though Cardinal Wyszyński was not specific as to the reason for his absence, Pius let it be known clearly enough that he believed the reason was Poland's Communist regime.[7]

Early in his last year of life, Pius raised several young priests to the rank of bishop. One of them was a Fr. Karol Wojtyła, whom he made Auxiliary Bishop of Kraków. The news reached Fr. Wojtyła while on a kayaking trip with several of his parishioners and other lay members of his circle. A phone rang in a nearby town, and the message as it got through was simply Cardinal Wyszyński needs to speak with you.[8] Wojtyła would not be able to tell, just from that, what it was all about. For all he knew, this being Communist Poland before de-Stalinization, he might have been under arrest. Instead, he was under a miter. Only Pius XII could have told him which was worse.

YOU BE THE JUDGE:

Did the Soviet Union plot to tarnish the reputation of Pope Pius XII and the Church?

What follows is not the whole story, but it so dominates discussion of Pius XII that it merits being dealt with at adequate length.

During and after World War II, Pius XII was widely praised for his work on behalf of peace and justice, including, specifically, his efforts on behalf of the Jews. The turning point in public opinion of Pius XII and the Holocaust started in 1963 with the performance and publication of a play by Rolf Hochhuth called *The Deputy* (*Der Stellvertreter*, perhaps more accurately The Placeholder, or The Representative, or even The Vicar), which centered on Pius and portrayed him as morally insensitive toward—even supportive of—the mass killing of Jews.

It may seem unlikely that a single play would have as much influence as *The Deputy* did, even though it quickly traveled to the stages of London and New York. But several other factors may have contributed to its influence. The play takes seven hours to perform: the theory of cognitive dissonance would suggest that anyone who sits through a play that long will conclude that there is at least "something to it." Furthermore, 1963 was the second year of Vatican II—a time when world media were already focused on a media-promoted narrative in which a new "good" Church, now on its second new pope, contrasted with a recently ended "bad" Church, and Pius XII was associated with the latter. Of note, too, is that the Jerusalem trial of Adolf Eichmann in 1961 riveted world attention on the Holocaust. The trial of Eichmann, who more than any other actually carried out the murders, would have undermined Hochhuth's thesis: at one point the chief prosecutor, Gideon Hausner, said, "The pope himself intervened personally on behalf of the Jews of Rome."

Perhaps the most shocking assault on Pius XII's reputation was made by Soviet Communists. Some authorities trace the Soviet plan to discredit Pius back to 1940, the second (and first full) calendar year of his pontificate and of the war—and a time when the Stalin-Hitler Pact was still in effect. But in 2007, Ion Pacepa, a Romanian, a former member of that country's dreaded Communist-era *Securitate*, and the highest-ranking defector ever from a Soviet-bloc security service, published in *National Review Online* an account of Soviet leader Nikita Khrushchev's secret campaign to undermine the moral authority of the papacy, with a special focus on Pius XII. According to Pacepa, this initiative began in 1960 and, though directed by the KGB, made heavy use of Romanian agents, including Pacepa. Inevitably, like *The Deputy* itself, Pacepa's article has spawned a subliterature of critique and defense. But see the subsection of Pacepa's article "The KGB produces a play." The director of the first production of *The Deputy* was the famous activist-director Erwin Piscator. Pacepa says the KGB was delighted to secure his services and deemed him a Communist and close to Moscow. Other secondary literature is split on whether Piscator was a Communist Party member or not, but all agree that he was a man of the Left who devoted his career to the idea that theater should be an agent of political change.

The Soviet Union had motive enough to target Pope Pius. Throughout the early postwar years, Italy's Communist Party was a political force to be reckoned with in national elections, and sometimes victorious in local ones. The Italian CP was in those days still Moscow-leaning enough (and Stalinist enough, while Stalin remained alive) that a national victory for it would have extended the Iron Curtain to the western Mediterranean, with the Vatican (to say nothing of Italy's medieval and renaissance cultural riches—and her people) on the wrong side. Pius XII's strong support for the Christian Democrats, a centrist party with Catholic influence, kept that from happening. Payback was due and, likewise, warnings to other leaders who might think of becoming nuisances to the Soviets.

Chapter 8

The Second Vatican Council

The College of Cardinals was rather depleted; there were only fifty-four cardinal-electors at the time. Two were kept from going to Rome by their Communist governments: Mindszenty of Budapest, Hungary, and Stepinac of Zagreb, Yugoslavia. Fifty-two. Then Cardinal Mooney of Detroit died of a heart attack in Rome just before the conclave started. Fifty-one. That meant the next pope could be elected with thirty-five votes: two-thirds plus one. The composition, however, of the college was considerably different from the one that met in 1939. With only seventeen participants, Italy's cardinals were at their lowest level of representation in five hundred years. Cardinal electors represented twenty-one countries (compared to sixteen), and twenty-one of them (not seven) were non-Europeans.

Some are surprised to learn that Cardinal Angelo Giuseppe Roncalli, the new pope John XXIII, served mostly as a diplomat until being appointed Patriarch of Venice. We tend to expect this pope, around whom swirl adjectives such as "pastoral," "smiling," and even the rather vague "good," to have been a pastor most of his career, as Bl. Pius IX and St. Pius X had been, but that was not the case. At the conclave before his election, two "conservative" cardinals, Ottaviani and Ruffini, met with Roncalli and expressed a hope. This is not uncanonical or even frowned upon, provided there is no quid pro quo and promises made. Ottaviani and Ruffini simply mused to Roncalli that it would be a very good idea for the Church to hold an ecumenical council.[1]

It didn't have to be Vatican II. The previous ecumenical council (1869–1870) was the first ever held at the Vatican, and that was due in part to the Holy See's uncertainty of safe proceedings anywhere else in Italy as the

Italian Kingdom was closing in on the capital city. Trent had been chosen for the great sixteenth-century council because it was in the Italian peninsula yet within the territory of the Holy Roman Emperor, whose buy-in was important. Before Trent, five ecumenical councils had been held at the Lateran (the pope's cathedral in his capacity as Bishop of Rome); two at Lyon, in France; and one each at Constance (Switzerland) and Florence. Pope John had options, but he chose the Vatican—no change of location but a change of number, as if to show that this council in some sense continued the previous one but in other ways differed from it.

Creating a link of place and name with Vatican I was not meaningless for Vatican II. Vatican I (as we have seen) dealt first with God himself (his knowability, within limits, by natural reason) and of course the papacy (by proclaiming, defining, and limiting papal infallibility). As a natural sequence, the next council would be expected to deal with the order of bishops, that of priests and religious, and the laity—and it did.

Between Vatican I and II, the "world" in which the Church works and evangelizes had changed, in many ways that should have been favorable. Recall that in 1869–1870, the Papal States were teetering on the abyss, and the pope was culturally besieged throughout Europe as well as almost literally besieged in Rome. In 1962, the Church was riding a height of prestige: there had been a Catholic literary renaissance, especially in the United States, but also in France; Thomism pulled weight in academia, the so-called neo-Thomists or Thomists of the Strict Observance were firmly ensconced in Roman dicasteries and most Catholic faculties of theology and philosophy; the reputation of the Church during the war had not yet been attacked (though that would soon start); Pope John was popular; and the United States had elected its first Catholic president.

That this entire edifice was balancing like a pencil on its well-sharpened point was not at all obvious to many. Cardinals Ottaviani, Ruffini, and Siri may have sensed it and thought a council was needed for what councils had always been used for: drawing lines and making distinctions. Some bishops and their *periti* (experts) came to Rome to rally around the pope and the Curia, but others came, it seems, for other reasons.

Most previous councils were like appellate judicial hearings, called to resolve an issue. Is the Son equal to the Father, as the Church had always taught, or was the increasingly popular doctrine of Arius right, which held that the Son is sort of top-deputy God, created by the (superior) Father? The Church held a Council at Nicaea in 325, to resolve this (outcome: Arius was wrong, the Son *is* equal to the Father). Vatican II, by contrast, was not called to resolve any doctrinal controversy.

As we saw in the chapter on Bl. Pius IX, Vatican I settled that the pope is infallible when formally addressing the entire Church in matters of faith of morals—but this had not been in much doubt. In this sense, Vatican I set a precedent for a council that would deal less with a particular doctrinal issue than with the state of the Church in a time of crisis brought on by the ever-shifting "modern world." On the other hand, it remains different from Vatican II in that, like most previous councils, it drew lines, and it offered a certain *défi* to the world outside the Church. Most of that world no longer thought the existence of God was provable: the smart set were agnostic or atheist, whatever they professed in public; believers were fideists, that is, they thought faith was necessary not only for truths knowable only by revelation (such as the Trinity, Jesus' divine sonship, and the atonement) but also for his very existence as benign creator.[2] And of course no one outside the Church thought the pope was infallible about *anything*.

Interestingly, while Pope John XXIII opened the council, he did not live to close it. In fact, he did not live long enough to publish a single one of the council's sixteen documents. John XXIII died in June 1963, and Cardinal Giovanni Battista Montini, Archbishop of Milan, was elected to the Chair of Peter less than twenty days later. Thus, John XXIII, who was widely reported to have said it was time to "throw open the windows of the Church" with the hope that an ecumenical council would foster a new Pentecost, left the bulk of the council's enduring work his successor, Paul VI.

Interpreting Vatican II

For better or worse, Vatican II is probably the most consequential internal event in the Catholic Church's twentieth century. Depending on what room you go into, the first debate you may hear about the council may be one about whether it was "only a pastoral council" or whether it taught in a way that commands the assent of Catholics. In another room you may hear the debate about whether the council is best interpreted via a "hermeneutic of continuity and reform" (as Pope Benedict XVI put it[3]) or a "hermeneutic of rupture."

These two disagreements should not be confused. But one strand of continuity is noticeable: a council that is solely pastoral (if there is such a thing) can in effect be ignored. It gives recommendations only. Moreover it must have a "sell-by date," because pastoral conditions change. Likewise, if it is an ongoing "event," its teaching is malleable. Popes and ecumenical councils (usually) issue doctrinal statements; events do not, even if they are "ongoing."

Vatican II was certainly pastoral, in that it avoided adding to the canon of infallible teachings, but *not* so as to be ripe for the shelf or the garbage. Pope Paul VI remarked in his general audience of January 12, 1966, barely a month after the close of the council,

> One may ask what was the authority, the theological qualification, that the Council wished to attribute to its teachings, knowing that it avoided giving solemn dogmatic definitions committing the infallibility of the ecclesiastic magisterium ... given the pastoral character of the Council, it avoided pronouncing and giving, in extraordinary mode, dogmas under the note of infallibility; but it nonetheless equipped its teaching with the authority of the ordinary supreme magisterium, which ordinary magisterium is so obviously authentic that it must be welcomed docilely and sincerely by all the faithful, according to the mind of the Council surrounding the nature and scope of the individual documents.[4]

You can't bowl it down the middle better than that. No, Vatican II was not a council like Nicaea, nor like the First Vatican Council. On one hand, it was a pastoral council with no new authoritative teachings. *On the other hand:*

1. Vatican II exercised the ordinary magisterium, which, no less than the extraordinary, demands "docile" and "sincere" reception by the faithful. (By the way, "docile" means teachable, not cringing or submissive.)

2. The individual documents of Vatican II, which are the only way in which a council speaks, carry their own "notes" of authority. If the council called it a "Dogmatic Constitution" (e.g., *Lumen Gentium*), that means, to put it nontechnically— you'd better listen! If it's a "declaration," there's a greater chance it's an adjustment to the pastoral situation of the age.

The hermeneutic of continuity has enemies on both "left"[5] and "right."[6] That is, those who welcome a complete overhaul of Catholicism say, with regard to Vatican II, nothing very different from those who deplore such an overhaul but believe it occurred and that Vatican II must therefore be rejected. Where the "middle" is depends on where the extremes are, and it looks very much as though the "hermeneutic of continuity" can claim the middle ground.

What Do We Need When We Need "Hermeneutics"?

While the dispute between hermeneutic of continuity and the hermeneutic of rupture or "event" goes on, another possible perspective asks why the council needs a "hermeneutic" at all. There is no dispute about the applicable hermeneutic (which just means interpretive mode, after all) for, say, Pius X's *Pascendi Dominici Gregis* or the encyclicals of Leo XIII or any of the great encyclicals of the centuries prior to 1960. They are plainly and obviously Catholic with many references to popes and documents before them to establish clearly in the mind of the reader that what is being taught has always and everywhere been taught. But it is unfortunately rare today that modern Church teaching and communications refer to or quote, in any meaningful way, Church documents prior to 1960. That there can even be a hermeneutical dispute about Vatican II says something about it.

One challenge is that the documents of Vatican II are committee work, and it shows. They are mostly longer than they need to be, with the possible exception of *Dei Verbum (Dogmatic Constitution on Divine Revelation)*. Paragraphs with different emphases display an effort to accommodate contradictory views; yet these end up not so much accommodated as confusingly uttered in parallel. They are also the work of men who, whatever their views or agendas, had an unlimited faith in "experts" and "commissions," wrote like "experts" on a "commission," and also spent a lot of word count recommending more commissions, with more experts. This recommendation was copiously followed in the immediate postconciliar period, sometimes with results it would be difficult to celebrate.

A "hermeneutic" of some kind is necessary in order to interpret such documents. Of the available options, this account will lean toward the "hermeneutic of continuity" for three reasons. First, as formulated by Benedict XVI, it accommodates "reform." Second, the theory emerges from John Henry Newman's *Essay on the Development of Doctrine*, which sets forth standards for distinguishing authentic development from deformity. Third, over two thousand years, continuity is a much more accurate way than rupture to describe what the Church actually does.

Sacrosanctum Concilium (Constitution on the Sacred Liturgy)

Ask the "average Catholic," "what did Vatican II do?" and you will get two answers: it got rid of Latin and it "turned the altar around." It actually did neither, though if you tilt your head and look at it just so, it may have unlocked doors through which both of these reforms entered brusquely after the council. Here is what *Sacrosanctum Concilium*, the council's Constitution on the Sacred Liturgy, its first document, said about Latin and the vernacular ("mother tongue"):

> 36. 1. Particular law remaining in force, the use of the Latin language is to be preserved in the Latin rites.[7]
>
> 2. But since the use of the mother tongue, whether in the Mass, the administration of the sacraments, or other parts of the liturgy, frequently may be of great advantage to the people, the limits of its employment may be extended. This will apply in the first place to the readings and directives, and to some of the prayers and chants, according to the regulations on this matter to be laid down separately in subsequent chapters.
>
> 3. These norms being observed, it is for the competent territorial ecclesiastical authority mentioned in Art. 22, 2, to decide whether, and to what extent, the vernacular language is to be used; their decrees are to be approved, that is, confirmed, by the Apostolic See. And, whenever it seems to be called for, this authority is to consult with bishops of neighboring regions which have the same language.
>
> 4. Translations from the Latin text into the mother tongue intended for use in the liturgy must be approved by the competent territorial ecclesiastical authority mentioned above.

There are five more references to "mother tongue" in the official Vatican English version, all of them suggesting liberality in its use. So is this a document decreeing that "particular law remain[s] in place" and that "Latin is to be preserved in the Latin [i.e., Western] rites"? Or is it a document that opens a wide door to vernacular liturgy by means of many little kicks on that door?

It rather depends on your hermeneutics. A continuitarian will see continued primacy of Latin—it will be, pardon the expression, the *ordinary form*—along with limited use of the "mother tongue," meaning vernacular may be introduced to make the scripture readings clearer. A rupturist will see a call to vernacularize the entire liturgy because the rupturist is reading this document not for *guidance* but for *permission*.

As for "turning the altar around"—demotic term for *versus populus* or "[the priest] toward the people," a practice replacing *ad orientem,* "toward the [liturgical] east" and facing the *same way the people are facing*—this is not directly addressed in *Sacrosanctum Concilium.* The council could have changed Pius XII's prohibition of *versus populus* in *Mediator Dei,* but in fact it did not, since *Sacrosanctum Concilium* says nothing clearly about this issue.

Still, the numerous differences between the Catholic experience of Sunday Mass prior to Vatican II and after the introduction of the *Novus Ordo* in 1969 are striking. In sum, it is difficult not to agree with historian Yves Chiron when he writes in his biographical sketch of key liturgical activist Annibale Bugnini,

> The critics who, after the adoption of the *Novus Ordo Missae* [Mass of Paul VI, 1969], said that the Council had never asked for a reform of the liturgy were wrong. On the other hand, it is true that the reform that Archbishop Bugnini had prepared and that Paul VI promulgated, went beyond what the Council had contemplated, if not what it had desired.[8]

Lumen Gentium (Dogmatic Constitution on the Church)

The second document of first-class importance is *Lumen Gentium (Dogmatic Constitution on the Church). Lumen Gentium*[9] is about the theology of the Church's structure. Among the documents of this pastorally minded council, *Lumen Gentium* is the only one besides *Dei Verbum* (on the sources of revelation) to bear the solemn designation "dogmatic constitution." Besides the episcopate, *Lumen Gentium* is also an overview of the priesthood, the laity as called to holiness equally with clergy and religious, and Our Lady as part of the structure of the Church.

Mystical Body/People of God

Lumen Gentium (*LG*) introduced the designation of the Church as the "people of God." This was received, and still is, as a relief after such heavy, Catholicy expressions as "mystical body of Christ" (e.g., in Pius XII's 1943 encyclical *Mystici Corporis*). "People of God" is the title of chapter 2 of *LG* and occurs *forty-one* other times in the document. It is certainly accurate (as is "mystical body"), but it remains surprising that, with representatives of other religions watching Vatican II so closely, the Church's co-optation of a term so closely associated with the Jewish people should have earned the Church such praise for co-opting it. Interreligious dialogue is mysterious.

Holiness Is Not Just for Those Who "Turn Pro"

The very idea that a priest, a monk, or a nun or sister has "turned pro" in the Church needs to be reexamined, according to *Lumen Gentium*'s chapters 4 and 5: on the laity, and on the universal call to holiness. The Church never taught that only those with visibly ecclesiastical vocations could attain holiness and become saints, but she had just possibly *forgotten* the universal call to holiness for a while. It's a dominant theme in St. Francis de Sales's *Introduction to the Devout Life* (1609). But with the copious flowering of new (if small) religious orders in the nineteenth century (in some respects a response to the French Revolution), and the canonizations of their founders, a habit of thinking crept into some circles in the Church (probably lay no less than clerical) that if you weren't a priest or a religious order member, you didn't have a chance. By the time of Vatican II, though, there were some voices arguing that lay folk too should imagine themselves on holy cards, qualifying for canonization, in a few cases even receiving it.

So why then are so many more priests and members of orders, especially founders, canonized than are lay people? Simple: Canonization requires, and should require, a lot of legwork—gathering writings, testimonies, interviews, evidence of local "cult," that is, devotion to the proposed *beatus* or saint—and a lot of people do that legwork. That puts founders of orders at the head of the line: all their members can chip in. Even a nonfounder member gets a boost. Diocesan clergy? Less so, but the resources of the diocese can be employed.

But how about a hypothetical person I'll call Mrs. McGillicuddy? I've made her up, but she stands in for a lot of real people. She raised ten kids who are all flourishing in marriages of their own, except for the two boys who became priests and the one daughter who became a cloistered Carmelite, and those three are fine too, thank you. Mrs. M did this despite the fact that her husband suffered economic setbacks, and to tell the truth was a bit free with the bottle, until Mrs. M—by gentle persuasion, not by nagging—helped him off it. She attended Mass daily. Her husband and children always felt free, but never coerced, to join her for the daily Rosary. She had sins, but given her habit of weekly confession, they didn't stand a chance. When she died, almost the whole parish came to the funeral, and everyone at the wake had a good-deed tale or funny story (because she was humorous too).

Who is going to do the work for her "cause"? Her kids, friends, and fellow Legion of Mary members will all help, but they are mostly busy laypeople too. For her cause to go forward, it will take a sympathetic local bishop (and Mrs. M was never a clerical suck-up) and officials in Rome who believe in lay sanctity. But ask a holy person and they'll tell you: beatification and canonization are not what it's about. Beatification and canonization are not achievement awards like an Oscar or the Pulitzer. But most of Mrs. McGillicuddy's many friends will already have sensed that. Though public cult cannot be offered to her before the Church says so, private devotion is permitted, and imitation is encouraged. In the meantime, there is All Saints Day. Still, we need to canonize more people like Mrs. McGillicuddy.

Up Close and Personal:

ARCHBISHOP FULTON J. SHEEN

Archbishop Fulton J. Sheen was a gifted theologian, teacher, and preacher who became known for his work on radio and television. Teaching at the Catholic University of America, he hosted the Catholic Hour on NBC radio for twenty years. He was appointed Auxiliary Bishop of New York in 1951 and moved to television with his Emmy-award-winning *Life Is Worth Living* program in 1952. It drew a weekly audience of up to thirty million. Sheen's final show, *The Fulton Sheen Program*, ran from 1961 to 1968 and was nationally syndicated. He is often said to be one of the first televangelists.

Sheen became the national director of the Society for the Propagation of the Faith in 1958 and served in that capacity for eight years before being transferred to the Diocese of Rochester. Author of more than seventy books, popular preacher, and brilliant scholar, Sheen was an object of envy both inside and outside the Church. He never spoke ill of anyone and bore the trials he faced graciously. The core of Sheen's spiritual life was a daily holy hour before the Most Blessed Sacrament, a practice he committed to on the day of his ordination and kept faithfully for the rest of his life. Archbishop Sheen died in 1979. Sheen's cause for beatification has been complicated by legal battles over his remains. His body was moved from St. Patrick's Cathedral in New York City to Peoria, Illinois, in 2019. While the necessary requirements for his beatification have been met, the date originally set for that event was suddenly and indefinitely postponed by the Vatican. As of this writing, a new date has not yet been determined.

Our Lady

What was the council to say about Mary? Pius IX had proclaimed the dogma of the Immaculate Conception in 1854, and Pius XII had proclaimed that of the assumption in 1950. What more needed to be said?

Some at the council hoped, as some do now, to see Mary proclaimed Mediatrix of All Graces, or even more strongly, Co-Redemptrix. We will wade into this quagmire only to note two things: the elements to support a Mediatrix proclamation are, arguably, already in place—and have been since the council of Ephesus in 431. There, Mary was proclaimed the Theotokos, or God-bearer. So, all graces come to us through Christ; then you add Ephesus (Mary is the Mother of God) and voilà! All graces come through Christ, and all of Christ comes through Mary, so all graces come through Mary. The transitive property supports "Mediatrix of All Graces."

Nevertheless, a teaching can be true and yet inadvisable. The very fact that a simple exercise of theological algebra leads to the doctrine actually cuts against making it the object of a special proclamation: the machinery of an infallible declaration is not generally cranked up for something the Church already teaches.

Yet such was not the reason given at Vatican II for remaining silent on both of these Marian teachings. The reason given was, rather, that it would slow down ecumenism. At the time, Protestant ecclesial communities and Eastern Orthodox Churches had sent official representatives to the council at the Holy See's official invitation. Catholic doctrine went into the council both strong and prestigious—so it seemed, anyway—and Pope John was not the only one who saw an ecumenical convergence on the horizon. And it looked like the "right" kind of ecumenism: "You-come-in-ism."[10]

Fifty-five years later, the world does not look the same. Eastern Orthodoxy is more badly split than ever,[11] and "liberal" Protestantism has ventured into moral swamps that would have seemed impossible in 1964. Therefore, Resolved: Ecumenism was a good reason to hold back on

Marian dogma at the council but no longer is. Even if "the house" "carries" that resolution, we are still left with what the council did and did not do.

There were almost certainly some at the council who wanted the word to go out that with their work, the Church was deemphasizing Our Lady and pulling the throttle back on Marian devotion.[12] Fr. de Lubac, near the beginning of the second volume of his council memoirs, drops the line "It is said that among those who insist on a separate schema on the Virgin, there is sometimes perhaps the desire to cut off any rapprochement with the East."[13] Such a document might have been very far from "cutting off rapprochement": Eastern Christians, Catholic and Orthodox, have a lively devotion to Our Lady. But de Lubac's offhand remark is a window to the early 1960s in the Church: stressing anything distinctive about Catholicism, or suspected of being so, was seen by influential theologians as hostile to the ecumenical hopes that were riding so high at that time.

So what *did* the council do about Our Lady? The council placed a chapter on Mary in its primary dogmatic constitution, thus situating her within the structure of the Church, because that is *Lumen Gentium*'s subject matter. Such an ecclesiological approach to Mary had never quite been achieved before. Whether it's the right way to teach about her at *all* times, it was the right way to teach about her at *that* time.

Remaining Documents

The documents of Vatican II offer instruction on a wide range of topics pertinent to the Christian life, including missionary activity, life in the clerical, religious, and lay states, the Church's relationship to non-Christian religions, religious freedom, and Christian education. While the content of the faith was reaffirmed, Council Fathers chose to speak in a tone that was warmer and less strident. They did so largely because they were aware that modern communication had changed the audience. The documents of Vatican II were no longer internal memos written for chanceries and seminaries. The Church was speaking to the world.

Among the remaining documents churned out by the council, *Dei Ver-bum* (*Dogmatic Constitution on Divine Revelation*) and *Gaudium et Spes* (*Pastoral Constitution on the Church in the Modern World*), are perhaps the most important. In *Dei Verbum*, the council reaffirmed that the Word of God flows to and through the Church in two streams: "Sacred tradition and Sacred Scripture form one sacred deposit of the word of God, commit-ted to the Church. . . . But the task of authentically interpreting the word of God, whether written or handed on, has been entrusted exclusively to the living teaching office of the Church, whose authority is exercised in the name of Jesus Christ" (*DV* 10). With *Gaudium et Spes*, the Church positioned herself as the ongoing presence of Christ in the contemporary world. Because "Christ . . . fully reveals man to man himself and makes his supreme calling clear" (*GS* 22), the Church exercises a unique role in the development of humanity as God created and envisioned it.

YOU BE THE JUDGE:

Isn't Vatican II universally hailed by theological liberals and disparaged by theological conservatives?

A blow-by-blow account of Vatican II is not possible here: not only for reasons of space but also because the historiography of the council is thoroughly laden with terms borrowed from sec-ular politics, which should not—yet constantly do—turn up in accounts of the council, scholarly as well as popular. The terms "liberal" and "conservative" are particularly prominent here, and particularly misleading. They naturally incline readers to project the "left" and "right" of their own national politics into the Church's frame of reference, where ideally they would have no meaning, and where in practice their meaning is at any rate much subtler than in the political sphere.

Perhaps every churchman should be "conservative," in the sense of taking seriously the duty to preserve, and to put forward anew the timeless doctrine of the Church, and perhaps every churchman should also be "liberal," in the sense of avoiding panicked overreaction to novel ways of expressing that doctrine and of stressing education over punishment when theologians go wrong, and perhaps also in the sense of reminding us that, while social service will never be the Church's primary mission, it is nonetheless an inseparable *part* of that mission.

But this irenic scenario has never played out since the concepts of "liberal" and "conservative," "left" and "right," became current. And since the 1960s take the blame for so much, let's cut them some slack here, widen the lens, and note that the imposition of human categories on the Church has been going on basically since the French Revolution. Everything was polarized after that. Thus, as we have seen, Pope Pius IX began his pontificate with sensible reforms that were called "liberal," but the then-existing European "left" soon showed its fangs in Rome, and after 1848 Pius saw conservation as his mission, and so became highly "conservative." Leo XIII in *Rerum Novarum* defended the rights of workers, yet also defended private property and rejected socialism, so was he balancing "liberal" and "conservative," or is that somewhat reductionist? How about Pope Pius X? If one wants "liberal" or "progressive" credentials, it seems one must deny that there was even such a thing as Modernism; yet this denial prevents a discussion that could be fruitful, namely, on whether the actions of Pope Pius's allies were at all times the most judicious. And so on.

George Weigel is probably the closest we have to an umpire-like observer of the council. To this it will be objected that he is openly affiliated with conservative think tanks and journals. Nevertheless, his analysis of the council goes beyond "liberal" versus "conservative" score-keeping and tries to identify issues at stake that are not easily subject to politicization.

For example, to what extent was the council about "who's in charge" issues? Who's in charge—the pope? National bishops' conferences? The laity? Parish committees? Activist/interest groups? Did the council mean to focus on these questions? And if it did, what did it decide? Or was it about reenergizing the Church for an evangelizing mission that had become different than it had been before? It takes a mind far gone in activism to shoehorn these questions into a "liberal"/"conservative" framework.

Weigel once remarked (and has made a similar point on many occasions) that John XXIII "did not intend to set off a twenty-five-year cat and dog fight about who's in charge in the Catholic Church." Rather, "he intended his Council to be a Pentecostal experience that as he put it in his opening address to the Council would impel throughout the Church a new sense of missionary or as we would say today, evangelical vitality."

There cannot be a better place to *begin* looking for the meaning of the Second Vatican Council than in the pope's public declarations of what he meant for it. After that, meaning can be found in the form of its final written declarations that were approved and promulgated by Pope Paul VI.

Chapter 9

Civil Unrest and the Return of Radicalism

Vatican II closed in 1965. The years immediately following were tumultuous. Berlin was a divided city. Soviet and Chinese communist regimes were aggressively expanding their spheres of influence. Maoist riots in Paris almost brought down the Fifth Republic and birthed a generation of cultural-revolutionary sleeper-cell activists known as soixante-huitards ("Sixty-Eighters"). The United States was reeling with Woodstock's culture of drugs and "free love," the long-overdue civil rights movement, and violent antiwar protests. The rise of Soviet-funded and trained "national liberation fronts" led violently to new, nominally "nonaligned" nations. The arms race and the space race were both in full force. Global social forces facilitated the rise of coercive population control policies.

False Promises

While the council was in session (October 11, 1962–December 8, 1965), the rumor mill was working overtime. Much of what went around was motivated by fear, no doubt; some, however, was wishful thinking. What did people wish for? It depended a lot on whether they considered ecumenical councils as agents of change or guardians of continuity. Ah yes, the hermeneutics again. Suffice it to say that a significant number of Catholics began to hope that the council would ditch celibacy, allow married priests in the Latin rite, and embrace at least some of the sexual revolution and abandon its prohibition of artificial contraception.

Of course, more "liberal" elements within the Church, who may well have had a role in stirring up these expectations, were happy to make use of them. When neither of these changes materialized, the number of unhappy campers was significant. But they were not alone. On the opposite side of the Catholic spectrum, traditionalists were also disappointed in Vatican II, and more than a few sought out places where they could hold onto the faith as they knew it.

Paul VI and *Humanae Vitae*

The polarization of Catholics after the council was most visible in 1968, when Pope Paul VI published *Humanae Vitae (On Human Life)*. In contrast to the Protestant churches, which by this time had all endorsed or allowed for contraception, Paul VI reaffirmed the Church's teaching on sexual morality and the procreative purpose of sex. It was a nail in the coffin for those within the Church who advocated a Catholic version of the sexual revolution that had been underway since the 1920s.

We can almost certainly say that Pope Paul VI was shocked by the global cultural revolution of (roughly) 1967–1973, a span bookmarked by the American Catholic colleges' declaration of independence from Church authority (the "Land O' Lakes statement") and *Roe v. Wade* and *Doe v. Bolton*, the US Supreme Court decisions that attempted to settle the abortion debate by awarding pro-abortion forces a near-total victory. In between those bookends came the highly organized and well orchestrated internal Church revolt against *Humanae Vitae*, yet taking Pope Paul by surprise in both its extent and hostility.

Up Close and Personal:

MOTHER TERESA OF KOLKATA

Agnes Bojaxhiu was born in Skopje, then part of the Ottoman Empire, in 1910. Her father was active in Albanian community politics and died when she was eight years old. There is evidence that he may have been murdered. The family was plunged into financial instability.

Agnes was intrigued by stories of missionaries, and by the time she was twelve, she had become convinced that she should commit herself to religious life. She left home in 1928 to join the Sisters of Loreto in Ireland. She arrived in India at eighteen and began her novitiate in Darjeeling. There, she learned Bengali and taught at a local school. Sr. Teresa took her solemn vows in Kolkata (Calcutta) in 1937. She taught at the Loreto convent school for girls for almost twenty years and was appointed headmistress in 1944.

Over the years, Sr. Teresa became increasingly sensitive to the poverty that surrounded the school. When she traveled to Darjeeling by train for her annual retreat in 1947, she received what she later referred to as "the call within the call," a vocation to serve the poorest of the poor while living among them. Teresa began her ministry among the slums of Kolkata in 1948. She wore sandals with a white and blue sari, became an Indian citizen, and spent several months receiving basic medical training.

Without financial support, Sr. Teresa begged for what she needed. She was joined by a few young women in 1949 and received permission to leave Loreto and found what would become the Missionaries of Charity. Her work centered on care for the destitutes who were dying in the streets. Eventually, she opened numerous houses for the dying, orphanages, schools, clinics, AIDS shelters, and more. The community that began with twelve members now has more than 4,500 religious sisters and is active in 133 countries.

Recognized as one of the era's great humanitarians, Mother Teresa received the Nobel Peace Prize in 1979. She had a reputation for being tough underneath her contagious smile and was known for saying, "There are no great things, only small things with great love." However, personal letters written by Mother Teresa (published as *Come, Be My Light* in 2007) reveal a completely different and unexpected side of the four-foot-ten powerhouse of selfless charity. While she dedicated her life to bringing the love of Christ to the world's least, she experienced little of that love herself. For more than fifty years, Mother Teresa served God with little sense of his presence and riddled with darkness and doubt. She was canonized in 2016.

Last Years

Throughout the mid-1970s, Pope Paul VI was visibly weak. His lack of media impact during his last years was, perhaps, a measure of this. *National Review* (*NR*), the flagship conservative magazine in the United States, with a strong Catholic influence, later criticized his "nodding reign." But *NR* needs to be taken with a grain of salt when commenting on Church matters, and "nodding" conveys some but not all of the later Paul VI era.

Internal dissent, which claimed a mandate from Vatican II but was unable to point to any of its decrees, was tearing the Church apart. In 1965, the opening of the door to liturgical reform had led to an instant liturgical revolution, requiring Paul's intervention with the encyclical *Mysterium Fidei*. Similarly, the council, relabeled and reconceptualized as the "spirit of Vatican II," unleashed forces that Pope Paul did not intend, did not condone, but could not combat—except perhaps by suffering.

A list of his encyclicals and other major statements shows them crowded into the pre-1970 part of his pontificate. The "pop-Catholic" grapevine, for what it's worth, has ever after been full of whisperings that the pope undertook extraordinary mortifications for the Church. That he wore a hair shirt during Lent is only the beginning. And while exaggerations are likely, that he suffered terribly for the Church, through voluntary as well as (inevitable) involuntary means, seems certain. For example, he had severe arthritis during his later years; while not as moving a story as the hair shirts (which may also be true), it certainly gave Paul VI pain that he could offer up. Perhaps Paul VI realized that there was little he could do now for the Church except suffer for her. And he did do that until his death in 1978.

The Year of Three Popes

The conclave of August 1978 was primarily a contest between the "conservative" Cardinal Siri, who had also been a candidate in 1958 and 1963, and a group of cardinals who appear to have divided the "liberal" vote among them. Between the two groups, Albino Luciani, Patriarch of Venice, yet unknown outside of Italy, and in Italy known mainly for his book *Illustrissimi*, a whimsical collection of "letters" he wrote to long-dead or fictional characters, was a very strong second choice. No doubt helped by his famous smile, Luciani drew from every faction, except (per conclave rules) himself.

It cannot be said that Luciani's thirty-three days as pope were without consequence. First, he rejected a coronation—thus making it unlikely for future popes to have one, unless they are willing to face media ridicule for reviving a tradition long associated with the office. Apparently eager to show continuity with both Pope John and Pope Paul, Luciani also broke new ground by taking a double name: John Paul. Normal papal protocol would hold that a pope who breaks in a new name is known by that name alone, without a numeral. But John Paul, again breaking with tradition, insisted throughout his thirty-three days that he was John Paul the First, not just John Paul. These tics made John Paul I seem like a radical; yet others said at the time and shortly after that it was on his agenda to restore the pre–Vatican II liturgy and that he was even in contact with printers about carrying this out without noticeable delay.

There are several rumors about the kind of pope John Paul I would have been if he had lived longer. During the gestational phase of *Humanae Vitae*, Luciani is said by some to have taken the view that "the pill" as it existed at the time was not a contraceptive (the Church has not agreed with him on this), but he did not challenge the central teaching against artificial birth control. Others suggest that he may have been planning a Tridentine liturgical revival. In any case, he was very anxious to heal the worsening breach with traditionalist archbishop Marcel Lefebvre. (By 1978, Lefebvre had illicitly ordained priests, but not bishops. This was not schismatic, merely rude.) But it is unlikely we will ever know more than we do now about John Paul I. With his thin record, captivating smile, and sudden death, he is the perfect blank slate on which partisans can draw their wishes.

Furthermore, having clocked the shortest pontificate ever, he is a natural target for conspiracy theories. The 1980s made a lot of undeserving millionaire-authors this way. Instead, we refer to the conclusion of heavily published journalists Gordon Thomas and Max Morgan-Witts: that Pope John Paul the First was not murdered but rather in very delicate coronary condition. He did not disclose his previous heart attacks to the conclave because nobody asked, and besides, he was on very reliable medication. There was just one problem: he had not brought his meds down with him from Venice, and in the excitement that followed, he forgot to send for them. So he died of a heart attack.

The papal entourage made things worse by rearranging his body, out of misplaced embarrassment that he had been found at room temperature by a nun-assistant, who happened to be the first one in the papal household to sound reveille that morning. But often in the past, popes had trusted nuns as part of their immediate entourage; there would have been nothing wrong with complete candor in this case, and for certain, more scandal was caused by this cover-up than would have been caused by the unvarnished truth.

So back to Rome came the cardinals. This time, even though the heat had receded a little since August, they were not happy about the primitive accommodations within the Vatican. "Rooms" for cardinal-electors were often created by putting up folding screens in Vatican offices and hallways. The head? It's down the hall. Once every fifteen or twenty years, cardinals could put up with this for the sake of the "wow" factor in electing a pope, but twice in six weeks was pushing it.

In discussing the second conclave of 1978, we may as well start with Cardinal Franz König of Vienna. Going back to the council, he had a long reputation as a moderate "liberal," but Thomas and Morgan-Witts report that he decided, by October, that his good friend and fellow council father, Cardinal Karol Wojtyła, was the right man. He encouraged him to accept if elected. "And," he added, "you must take the name John Paul II." König began talking up Wojtyła. He received immediate support from his long-time mentor, Cardinal Stefan Wyszyński, Archbishop of Warsaw. Philadelphia's Cardinal Krol, a fellow Pole, went over to Wojtyła as well, bringing some American votes with him. Wojtyła was elected on the eighth scrutiny.

"*Un polacco?!*" Romans in the Piazza began asking each other. This term is not a slur in Italian, but it did reflect the bewilderment in the crowd. The papacy was an Italian institution! How had they found an Italian in Poland? But when John Paul II appeared on the balcony and said, "If I make a mistake in your—that is, our—Italian, you will correct me," he won them over right away.

YOU BE THE JUDGE:

Doesn't the Church oppose feminism?

To be fair, it matters what *kind* of feminism we are considering. The Church does not support feminism that denies the complementarity of the sexes, embraces "gender theory," or aligns itself with artificial contraception or abortion. However, throughout history, the Catholic Church has been an advocate for raising the status of women. The Church has championed women's rights to education, to work, and to equal pay.

Over the centuries, numerous Catholic women have been celebrated for their achievements in diverse fields. In the Modern Era, the contributions of Catholic women include those of Marie Curie (chemist); Mother Henriette DeLille (free woman of color who founded Sisters of the Holy Family for free women of color); Maria Montessori (first woman doctor in Italy, founder of the Montessori method of education); Flannery O'Connor (American Catholic fiction writer); Sigrid Undset (Norwegian convert and winner of the Nobel Prize in Literature); Dorothy Day (journalist and social activist); Sister of Charity Mary Kenneth Keller (the first woman to earn a PhD in computer science); and Thea Bowman (religious sister who ministered primarily to fellow African Americans). Canonized saints include St. Edith Stein (a feminist scholar), St. Gianna Beretta Molla (a pediatrician), St. Josephine Bakhita (a formerly enslaved religious sister), St. Katharine Drexel (university and religious order founder), St. Frances Xavier Cabrini (sister who served immigrants), St. Marianne Cope (missionary to Hawaii), and St. Zélie Martin (owner of a successful home business and the mother of St. Thérèse of Lisieux).

Chapter 10

A Culture of Life

"John Paul the Great"? The title has not been made official; such a title for popes never is. The Holy See recognizes saints through the process of beatification and canonization. The addition of "the Great" is given by long custom, but it is recognized in the *Annuario Pontificio*, an official Vatican personnel directory/almanac/phonebook. With classic Vatican sprezzatura and indifference to time, the popes are listed there—with all the "Greats" so designated: Leo I (reigned 440–461), Gregory I (reigned 590–604), and Nicholas I (reigned 858–867).

What makes St. John Paul II a candidate for the title, and "great" whether it eventually settles on him or not, is that he was called to the Petrine office at a time of deep confusion. His scholarly work did much to bridge the gap between traditional, rationalistic, scholastic Thomism and the "turn to the subject" ("phenomenological") Thomism of Poland's University of Lublin. With this synthesis, he renewed the faith of many Catholics and drew in many new ones.

A Vatican II Father who grew up under each of the twentieth century's two great totalitarianisms, and led a major archdiocese under one of them, Pope John Paul II was above the "first world problems" that fueled both "liberal" and "conservative" factions in the West. Those factions were almost unknown in Eastern Europe. There, because of poverty and hostile Communist domination, the Churches (plural because the Eastern Orthodox suffered too) had first and foremost to survive, not to argue over where the tabernacle should be, or whether there'd be altar girls, or whether Latin was still required or had been forbidden, or what the powers of the bishops' conferences were. While negotiating for survival, the persecuted Church stayed rooted in its apostolic mission, something that seems to have eluded the Church in less troubled places.

As Archbishop of Kraków, Karol Wojtyła wrote a book, *Sources of Renewal*, on the implementation of Vatican II in his archdiocese. If you're looking for a clerical procedural manual on turning altars around, you'll need to look elsewhere. *Sources of Renewal* is as philosophical as most of this man's work, and it shows a conception of Vatican II as a preparation of the Church for battles to come—hardly the way the council is usually thought of in the West.

Much of John Paul II's pontificate would be devoted to explaining Vatican II. In a sense, the council was not closed until a pope came along who could explain it, one who not only had participated in it but also was in a position to understand it free from Western (and South American) "left" and "right" interpretive shackles.

Poland: "We Want God!"

Popes travel; it's not that remarkable anymore. But that is largely because of John Paul II. He not only revived the practice; he appears to have institutionalized it. John Paul II eventually visited 129 countries, but his first trip as pope was to a very special place. A pontifical trip to his native Poland meant facing down numerous obstacles. The Communist, Soviet-satellite dictatorship maintained its official atheism (derived from Marx and maintained by Soviet ideology). Polish officials had been alarmed at the election of one of its citizens as pope and were determined to prevent the visit or at least make it difficult.

John Paul's suggestion of a two-day visit for early May 1979, to coincide with the Feast of St. Stanislaw of Kraków on May 7, was refused by Communists because they didn't want a distraction from May Day, an international workers' holiday that Communism had appropriated. The counteroffer was for nine days in June! The Church in Poland said yes, thank you—and promptly moved the Feast of St. Stanislaw for that year to June.

John Paul's first event was an outdoor Mass in Warsaw's "Victory Square," a frequent scene for regime rallies and well-organized "spontaneous demonstrations." In his homily, the pope reiterated the *Gaudium et Spes/Redemptor Hominis* doctrine: Christ reveals man, to man. Throughout the trip John Paul said nothing overtly political, but if Christ definitively reveals to man what man is, then Marx can't have done so, nor any regime based on the theory that man is a purely economic (or racial) being. At the end of the homily, since the days were drawing close to Pentecost, he asked for an outpouring of the Holy Spirit on Poland. At this, Massgoers and pilgrims began chanting "We want God!" A million pilgrims attended his Mass at Jasna Góra, that is, the shrine of Our Lady of Częstochowa. Two million showed up for his closing Mass at the town center of Kraków, his former archdiocese.

This success came in spite of Polish state authorities telling schoolteachers to characterize John Paul as an "American"-style politician and television crews to focus only on priests, nuns, and old folks at the papal Masses, not on young people and certainly not on young families. It came in spite of Soviet and East German agents within the clergy trying to sabotage the visit in ways both high concept (influencing media coverage) and low (misdirecting buses carrying pilgrims). In the end, fully a third of all Poles had seen the pope in person.

John Paul II's journey to Poland in 1979 was, some believe, the beginning of the end of Communism in Europe. It was not for economic reasons (though that system obviously lagged behind the free market as a generator of wealth and in its failure to achieve economic justice out of any wealth it did create or allow), but for religious ones. The regime had said, over and over, "No God." The people had answered, "We want God!"

Theology of the Body

Between September 1979 and November 1984, Pope John Paul gave 129 teachings that constitute (along with his previous work *Love and Responsibility*) what has come to be known as "Theology of the Body." Astute philosopher that he was, John Paul joined Thomism with the personalism of modern phenomenology. He examined human sexuality in the larger context of the divine plan for human love, affirming the dignity of the human person as one who is an end to be loved rather than a means to be used. As such, John Paul fleshed out, as it were, the twofold purpose of sex as both procreative in children and unitive in mutual self-gift. This innovation in pastoral and practical theology stresses the complementarity of man and woman, and calls each to a free and total gift of self not only in marriage but also in single, celibate, and religious vocations.

Dissenting Theologians

In the decade prior to John Paul II's election, academics bearing the title and credentials of Catholic theologians were teaching dissenting views, contrary to their contracts and the requirements of their "mandatum" to teach in the name of the Church. In addition, they were becoming media lions for doing so.

Theology is faith seeking understanding in the service of the Truth, not investigative sophistry in service to the zeitgeist. But without a pope willing to explain this and enforce it—more forcefully than Paul VI had done—the result is scandal in the most technical and urgent sense: creating obstacles to the Faith. This is all the more so when Church teaching contradicts the prevailing popular and elite opinions of the era, and a dissenting theologian demands to be considered courageous for saying merely what the surrounding culture says.

For these reasons, it was a source of scandal that Fathers Hans Küng, Charles Curran, and Leonardo Boff were in official teaching positions in the Church. John Paul II restored the credibility of the Church by taking a stand and taking action. Küng rejected distinctly Catholic doctrines in an effort to heal divisions created by the Protestant Reformation. He rejected papal infallibility outright and denied the virgin birth of Christ. The Vatican's move against Küng in December 1979 was moderate almost to the point of absurdity, but that did not stop worldwide pearl clutching about the alleged revival of the Inquisition. Küng was not defrocked, his degree was not revoked, and he did not even have to stop teaching at Tübingen. He was deprived only of the right to teach in the official capacity of a Catholic theologian.

Charles Curran had participated vigorously in the well-organized dissent from *Humanae Vitae* as soon as it came out. Starting with the contraception issue, Curran soon became a full-spectrum denier of Catholic teaching on sexual ethics, while a professor of moral theology at Rome's and the bishops' own official university, the Catholic University of America (CUA). Over the course of a correspondence throughout 1985, the Congregation of the Doctrine of the Faith asked Curran if he would kindly teach Catholic faith without dissent, which after all, was his job as a theologian at Catholic University; yet he kept declining to do so. In July 1986, Curran was notified that the Holy See would inform CUA that he was no longer suited for the post of teaching Catholic moral theology there. As in the Küng case, Curran was not defrocked, not forbidden to make media appearances, and not even forbidden to publish. But teaching moral theology at a Catholic university? No, to do that, you actually have to teach Catholic morality.

Leonardo Boff, a Franciscan from Brazil, was and is a proponent of "liberation theology." Using a Marxist analysis, it proposes the belief that Christ's gift—our liberation from sin and citizenship in his kingdom— goes hand in hand with liberation from oppressive governments and social structures. In its more extreme form, Christ and the Gospel became mere metaphors for Marxist revolution. Between 1984 and 1986, John Paul II's Holy See, through Cardinal Joseph Ratzinger's Congregation for the Doctrine of the Faith, issued two successive statements on liberation theology. Liberation theologians reacted in different ways. Boff was only asked to stay quiet for a year and reflect. He did not and, after a second admonition in 1992, resigned from the Franciscans.

The point with all of these cases was not to punish the dissidents but to show there is truth in advertising: you can't say your product is Catholic when it's not. The French wine industry with its *appellations contrôlées* gets this. John Paul II restored to the Church her necessarily restricted appellation.

Meanwhile, for uncountable numbers of people inside the Church or those considering coming inside, a sign was sent: the Church would not only teach but also stand up for its teachings. Paul VI had left the latter somewhat in doubt. John Paul II resolved it.

An Assassination Attempt

On May 13, 1981, the sixty-fourth anniversary of the beginning of the apparitions of Our Lady at Fatima, Portugal, Turkish criminal and drifter Mehmet Ali Agca fired two shots at Pope John Paul while he was greeting pilgrims in St. Peter's Square. One bullet was deflected off the pope's thumb and elbow and injured two American tourists, to whom John Paul later sent blessings. The other bullet did great damage in his gut, but missed his abdominal artery. Had this been struck, doctors are convinced he would have bled out during the transfer from the popemobile to the ambulance. Others must interpret this as their faith and judgment direct, but John Paul never had the slightest doubt that he had been saved by the Blessed Virgin Mary under her title of Our Lady of Fatima. "One hand fired the bullet, another guided it," he later said.

Even so, he was in grave danger during the ambulance trip. (The Gemelli Clinic, which is set up to handle papal medical emergencies, is about four miles away from Vatican City, and it was Roman rush hour when the ambulance was en route. Biographer George Weigel says it is normally a twenty-five-minute drive; the ambulance made it in four, which if you've experienced Roman drivers, conjures up quite a scene.)

John Paul remained conscious through the ambulance trip but was quickly losing blood and blood pressure. At the Gemelli, he passed out as they were prepping him for surgery. His ever-present secretary, Fr. Stanislaw Dziwisz, gave him the last rites. Recovery was a slow, two-steps-forward-one-step-back process.

Agca's motive and the identity of his handlers, if any, for this crime remain controversial. But thanks to investigative journalist Claire Sterling, near certainty has clustered around the view that Agca was being "run" by the Soviet bloc—that is, the Soviet Union itself—acting through its very obedient tools, the secret service of the People's Republic of Bulgaria.

For one thing, for the two years prior to the assassination attempt, Agca was jet-setting in a way that was beyond his family poverty and lack of visible financial means. For another, he had been convicted in Turkey for the 1979 assassination of a highly regarded newspaper editor but had escaped. Moreover, the period from December 1980 to May 1981 had been one of heightening tension between the Soviet bloc and the papacy. In December 1980, as Solidarity, the first independent trade union in the supposed workers' states of the Soviet bloc, rejoiced in its newfound existence and legitimacy among dockworkers, the Soviet Union was detected massing troops near its Polish border. They perhaps thought the United States, in transition from the Carter to the Reagan administrations, would not be able to coordinate a response. But strong messages to stand down came from both the US and from John Paul.

The Soviets stood down in ill humor, summoning senior Polish officials to Moscow to impress upon them that they would have to do something about Solidarity if the USSR didn't. The Soviets were then free to concentrate on their invasion of Afghanistan; they denounced the free Ukrainian Catholics as Nazis, and they were really, really mad at John Paul II. Yuri Andropov, KGB chieftain and soon to be successor to the decrepit Brezhnev, was in on the meetings. But the KGB did not need to risk exposure when it could just as well work through Bulgaria's Dăržavna Sigurnost (State Security). The Dăržavna Sigurnost could surely handle the pope assignment. And so Agca acquired a Bulgarian gun and several Bulgarian friends in both Sofia and Rome. This much was established from his confused and self-contradictory interrogation in Rome.

The court sentenced Agca to life in prison. John Paul visited him there in 1983. Their conversation was private, but John Paul wanted the fact of it to be known and so invited photographers to get a picture of himself and Agca, sitting as equals in plastic seats in a corner of the cell. The only words the media heard were the pope (whose many languages did not include Turkish) asking Agca, "Do you speak Italian?" Agca nodded, and they continued conversing, privately, for about twenty minutes. John Paul gave Agca a rosary, and they shook hands upon parting.

Despite the life sentence passed on Agca, John Paul successfully petitioned the president of Italy to pardon him in 2000. Agca was then deported to Turkey to finish his prison term for the assassination of the newspaper editor. He was released in 2010. He caused a stir four years later when he traveled to Rome, again, and tipped off the media that he would be laying flowers on John Paul's tomb.

The near brush with death led John Paul to do in 2000 what several of his predecessors could have done but chose not to: reveal the Third Secret of Fatima (see Up Close and Personal: The Message of Fatima in chapter 4 for more information). Some say Pope John XXIII read it, decided not to reveal it, and instead called the Second Vatican Council.

The Extraordinary Synod and the Catechism of the Catholic Church

Early in 1985, John Paul announced an extraordinary session of the Synod of Bishops "to celebrate, verify, and promote" Vatican II on its twentieth anniversary. Since the resolution of the status of certain high-visibility dissident theologians was by then a known fact, many news outlets assumed this was code for "reversing" the council.

Today, observers notice that cardinals such as Godfried Danneels and Walter Kasper had influential roles at the Extraordinary Synod. As these churchmen were later revealed to have rather extreme views, and Danneels was revealed to have helped cover up clergy sexual abuse in his diocese of Mechelen-Brussels, it is assumed that the Extraordinary Synod accomplished nothing of value. This is wrong.

At a minimum, the Extraordinary Synod pierced the veil of immunity from criticism that had descended on the postconciliar Church. Perhaps lacking confidence in the council itself, many churchmen fell into considering any criticism of the subsequent era pointing out that certain things had gone badly wrong to be an attack on the council itself and therefore off limits. But John Paul had been a Council Father, and his increasingly visible assistant, Cardinal Ratzinger, had been a council peritus (reporting to Cardinal Frings, back then Archbishop of Munich-Freising). The Extraordinary Synod was in the hands of friends of Vatican II—not enemies—but friends who did not necessarily interpret it as, say, the *New York Times* would have recommended.

The Extraordinary Synod recognized that much had gone wrong, especially in catechesis and doctrinal awareness. At the time, the Church's only official universal catechism was the one prepared in the sixteenth century, largely by St. Charles Borromeo and issued by the authority of Pope Pius V. This one is still in print, and still authoritative, which we know because the new one quotes from it extensively. Vatican II itself had not called for writing a catechism—probably a shrewd move at the time. But by 1985 the need was great, and the time was right, for a new one. This proposition was first placed on the synod floor by Cardinal Hyacinthe Thiandoum, of Dakar, Senegal. It was seconded the next day by Boston's Cardinal Bernard Law.

The *Catechism of the Catholic Church* came out in 1992, in a draft version in French. Over the next few years it came out in a Latin *editio typica* and in many other languages. Many people had said for years that all had not gone well, or even as the council intended, in the implementation of the council. The difference the 1985 synod made was that one could now say this "out loud," so to speak, without being labeled as an "enemy of the council."

Liturgy: The Failed SSPX Outreach, the Successful Indult

"I almost spilled my coffee," one liturgist at Georgetown was quoted as saying one morning in 1984. What had caused this reaction? Pope John Paul had issued, through the Congregation for Divine Worship, the "circular letter" *Quattuor Abhinc Annos*, subtitled *Indult for the Use of the Roman Missal of 1962*. This was the last edition of the Traditional Latin Mass, sometimes called the Tridentine Mass (though most of it is much older than the Council of Trent), the older usage preceding the introduction of the Novus Ordo Missae at Advent of 1969.

For those paying attention, the indult order did not come out of the blue. In 1980 (hence the letter's title, which means "four years ago"), barely into his pontificate, John Paul had solicited reports concerning how the New Mass had been received and difficulties in, even resistance to, its reception. *Quattuor* leads with this fact.

The core of *Quattuor* reads, "The Supreme Pontiff, in a desire to meet the wishes of these groups grants to diocesan bishops the possibility of using an indult whereby priests and faithful, who shall be expressly indicated in the letter of request to be presented to their own bishop, may be able to celebrate Mass by using the Roman Missal according to the 1962 edition."

So let us take a step back. From 1970 to 1984, the Traditional Latin Mass came as close as it ever came to being suppressed. Even so, it was not suppressed as such; rather, Paul VI ordained that the Missal of 1969, a.k.a. the Novus Ordo, be used instead. But long before 1984, requests for personal or regional indults were presented to Pope Paul, and according to legend, he never refused a single one. Thus, almost from the promulgation of the New Mass, English and Welsh bishops had permission to say the old one, or to authorize priests to say it, as a result of a request made by English Catholic writers and intellectuals, and some non-Catholics famous in the world of letters, such as Agatha Christie (hence the name "the Christie indult"). Furthermore, many individual priests petitioned

Paul for personal indults, and (again) according to legend, he denied none of them. So, 1970–1984 was not a period of absolute prohibition of the Old Mass but rather a time of scattershot indults, less organized than the one in 1984, but enough to restrain the claim that the Mass of Pius V was suppressed altogether.

On the basis of the 1984 indult, John Paul and Cardinal Ratzinger hoped to reconcile Archbishop Lefebvre and his Society of St. Pius X (SSPX) to the Church. At that point, the society was in disobedience (because of ordaining priests without permission, not because of using the old liturgy) but not yet in schism. However, the SSPX had issues with Vatican II other than liturgy (especially as regards religious liberty), and a reconciliation that was within sight in 1988 slipped away when Archbishop Lefebvre lost trust in the Holy See and went ahead with the unauthorized ordination of four bishops—a schismatic act, for the simple reason that bishops can consecrate, validly but illicitly, both priests and further bishops. This failure caused great grief to John Paul, and even more to Ratzinger, who had ridden point on the SSPX negotiations.

The tragedy of 1988 led, however, to John Paul's motu proprio *Ecclesia Dei* encouraging generous application of the indult, and to the creation and recognition of the Fraternal Society of St. Peter—priests who had formerly adhered to the SSPX but, at great personal cost, rejected schism. The FSSP and similar priestly societies have since become the nucleus of a Traditional Latin Mass revival that is not schismatic but fully inside the Church.

Up Close and Personal:

MORE SAINTS THAN EVER

The first saint to be formally canonized was St. Ulrich of Augsburg in 993, and by the twelfth century, the Church centralized— and officiated—the process. More recent popes have canonized saints in large numbers. John Paul II, for example, canonized

482 saints during the twenty-six years of his papacy. That's a lot when you realize there were only about three hundred canonizations in the previous six hundred years. This is partly due to the fact that Pope John Paul II streamlined the process in 1983. Martyrs used to require one posthumous miracle for sainthood, and nonmartyrs (who used to require four attested miracles) now require only two. Another reason may well be that recent popes have wanted to underscore the idea that holiness is possible for everyone—not just martyrs, priests, and religious—and in the circumstances of ordinary life.

The Great Encyclicals

John Paul II produced fourteen encyclicals over the course of his papacy. The three most important ones were written in the 1990s.

Veritatis Splendor (*The Splendor of the Truth*)

In continuity with scripture and tradition, approved theologians, and earlier papal magisteria, John Paul affirmed the reality of moral absolutes. In *Veritatis Splendor*, he carefully dismantles modern moral theologies known as "fundamental option," "consequentialism," and other "teleological" moral theories—so called because they make the "end" or goal (*telos*) of the actor, not of the act, determinative—all of which teach in some form that no act can separate us from God as long as, to put it colloquially, our "heart's in the right place." Against this, John Paul affirms the Church's ancient teaching, that there are intrinsically evil acts that, if chosen freely and with knowledge of their sinful character, are themselves acts of self-separation from God. The doors of the confessional remain open, but if such acts are done and not repented of, eternal loss is possible, even in someone still feeling friendly toward God.

In the last chapter, entitled "Lest the Cross of Christ Be Emptied of Its Power," John Paul includes a section on martyrdom.

> Countless other martyrs accepted persecution and death rather than perform the idolatrous act of burning incense before the statue of the Emperor (cf. Rev 13:7–10). They even refused to feign such worship, thereby giving an example of the duty to refrain from performing even a single concrete act contrary to God's love and the witness of faith. Like Christ himself, they obediently trusted and handed over their lives to the Father, the one who could free them from death (cf. Heb 5:7). .... Martyrdom, accepted as an affirmation of the inviolability of the moral order, bears splendid witness both to the holiness of God's law and to the inviolability of the personal dignity of man, created in God's image and likeness. This dignity may never be disparaged or called into question, even with good intentions, whatever the difficulties involved. Jesus warns us most sternly: "What does it profit a man, to gain the whole world and forfeit his life?" (Mk 8:36). (*VS* 91–92)

Evangelium Vitae (*The Gospel of Life*)

Next among the great encyclicals was *Evangelium Vitae*.

> Whatever is opposed to life itself, such as any type of murder, genocide, abortion, euthanasia, or wilful self-destruction, whatever violates the integrity of the human person, such as mutilation, torments inflicted on body or mind, attempts to coerce the will itself; whatever insults human dignity, such as subhuman living conditions, arbitrary imprisonment, deportation, slavery, prostitution, the selling of women and children; as well as disgraceful working conditions, where people are treated as mere instruments of gain rather than as free and responsible persons; all these things and others like them are infamies indeed. They poison human society, and they do more harm to those

> who practise them than to those who suffer from the injury.
> Moreover, they are a supreme dishonour to the Creator. (*EV* 3)

As this paragraph shows, *Evangelium Vitae* unfolds as a transideological critique of all trends that cheapen life, make its extinction easier, and make its maintenance and protection seem like burdens that no one may ask of an individual or of a society. Abortion was addressed, yes, but also contraception that regards the child potentially resulting from a sexual encounter as an enemy, as well as suicide and euthanasia, unnecessary wars, the arms trade, capital punishment, and large-scale social inequality that threatens destitution at its lower end without in any discernible way uplifting morality at the upper. No party or ideology can claim *Evangelium Vitae* as its manifesto; they can only measure themselves against it.

Fides et Ratio (*Faith and Reason*)

The last of what I am calling John Paul II's great encyclicals is *Fides et Ratio*. Conscious of the naming conventions for encyclicals, John Paul's first paragraph, here as in his other encyclicals and apostolic letters, gives this one its name and states its theme:

> Faith and reason are like two wings on which the human spirit
> rises to the contemplation of truth; and God has placed in the
> human heart a desire to know the truth—in a word, to know
> himself—so that, by knowing and loving God, men and women
> may also come to the fullness of truth about themselves (cf. Ex
> 33:18; Ps 27:8–9; 63:2–3; Jn 14:8; 1 Jn 3:2).

While opinionated but ignorant polemicists repeat Enlightenment and nineteenth-century tropes about how the Church is opposed to reason, John Paul makes clear that the Church is in the forefront of defending reason, and must be so in order to make theology comprehensible. In one chapter, "Credo ut intelligam" ("I believe in order that I may understand"), John Paul puts faith first. In the next, "Intellego ut credam" (the reverse), he hands the mic to natural reason. Deprived of reason, faith has stressed feeling and experience, and so runs the risk of no longer being a universal proposition. It is an illusion to think that faith, tied to weak reasoning, might be more penetrating; on the contrary, faith then runs the grave risk of withering into myth or superstition. By the same token, reason that is unrelated to an adult faith is not prompted to turn its gaze to the newness and radicality of being (sec. 48).

John Paul II did not call the Church to a precarious balance between Catholic tradition and post–Vatican II innovation. He called for restoration—but (and this is important) a restoration that remains in dialogue with adverse philosophies, as these themselves have developed from the origins of the revolution to current postmodernism:

> The currents of thought which claim to be postmodern merit appropriate attention. According to some of them, the time of certainties is irrevocably past, and the human being must now learn to live in a horizon of total absence of meaning, where everything is provisional and ephemeral. In their destructive critique of every certitude, several authors have failed to make crucial distinctions and have called into question the certitudes of faith.
>
> This nihilism has been justified in a sense by the terrible experience of evil which has marked our age. Such a dramatic experience has ensured the collapse of rationalist optimism, which viewed history as the triumphant progress of reason, the source of all happiness and freedom; and now, at the end of this century, one of our greatest threats is the temptation to despair. (Sec. 91)

The Apostolate of Suffering

John Paul II's final years were marked by a severe and publicly visible decline in his health: Parkinson's disease, a fall and a bad hip replacement, and just plain age. Well before the year 2000, several Catholic pundits who did not much like him predicted his imminent demise. He outlived them all. Not long after 2000, though, it was evident that he was in great pain most of the time. The *r* word (resignation) was in the air.

The point missed by those who suggested it was that Pope John Paul was serving the Church by suffering and witnessing to the value and dignity of every human life at every stage. Instead of resigning, John Paul added a fourth set of mysteries—the luminous—to the Rosary. Presiding over the Great Jubilee Year Two Thousand, Pope John Paul II ushered the universal Church across the threshold of the new millennium. He entered immortality April 2, 2005, on the vigil of Divine Mercy Sunday.

YOU BE THE JUDGE:

Didn't the Church completely mishandle clergy sexual abuse?

The short answer is yes. In the 1990s, a grim reality in the Church's life began to be noticed: some Catholic clergy were sexually abusing children—and not only children. Several arrests were made; then in 2002, a series of reports by the *Boston Globe* revealed the extent of the problem and the Church's inadequate response to it. As more information was brought to light, a number of disturbing facts came into view:

There was a "culture" of cover-up, and Church officials prioritized protecting "the Church's reputation" from scandal. Credible allegations of sexual abuse were handled privately. Victims and their families were often pressured to remain silent. Abusive priests were frequently reassigned or retired without explanation. Ironically, the Church's reputation is one of the things that has suffered most from the mishandling of these serious allegations.

Bishops placed excessive faith in psychological treatment. During the therapy-heavy era of the 1960s through the 1990s, sexual abuse was viewed by many prelates as sinful, but not criminal. Those who perpetrated it were considered to be suffering from an ailment that—numerous mental health professionals said—could be cured with proper treatment. Some of the treatment facilities on which bishops relied were outright fraudulent, but even the honest ones overpromised. Many of the offenders who were green-lighted by a treatment center were returned to active ministry without restriction and then "reoffended," an expression that conceals the suffering they inflicted.

The *Boston Globe*'s reporting led to the resignation of Boston's Cardinal Bernard Law for having frequently moved abusive priests from parish to parish. Despite Law's otherwise-sterling career as a civil rights activist, opponent of dissenting theology, and promoter and cotranslator of the 1992 *Catechism of the Catholic Church*, (see his obituary), he resigned in shame and spent his remaining years in Rome.

Victims of clergy sexual abuse were varied. Though the label "pedophile priests" was quickly slapped on the crisis, the implication that young children were the only victims was inaccurate. Psychologists consider it significant that most victims were above the age of puberty, and thus, most offenders on record were "ephebophiles" (or "pederasts") rather than "pedophiles."

Furthermore, as the case of Theodore McCarrick, ex-cardinal now removed from the clerical state, revealed in 2018, some abusers wielded their power within the Church to prey on seminarians. This leads to yet one more aspect of the crisis: though there have been female victims, a considerable preponderance of them have been male.

Homosexuality is, in some way, pertinent. It is clear that homosexual orientation does not make a person a sexual abuser. It is also clear that it is possible for both heterosexuals and homosexuals to live chastely. Nevertheless, it is also true that nearly 80 percent of clergy sexual abuse has been homosexual in nature.

Some observers of the scandal have gone to great lengths to exonerate homosexuality per se. Kenneth Woodward, for instance, argues that certain professions offer both authority and access to vulnerable minors: the priesthood as well as teaching and coaching. But even Woodward admits, "One cannot deny that homosexuality has played a role in the abuse scandals and their coverup, and to dismiss this aspect as homophobia one would have to be either blind or dishonest."

Perpetrators of clergy sexual abuse do not fit a single mold or pattern. Some of the credibly accused priests were sincere in their vocation but indulged moral failure that was inconsistent with their beliefs. Others led double lives: outwardly pious but secretly living in a way that is completely contrary to the teachings of the Church. For example, some members of the clergy have habitually engaged in sex—often promiscuous and homosexual—for decades.

The Catholic Church is no more likely to harbor sexual abusers than are other churches, public schools, secular private schools, and clergy of other religions. (There are numerous statistics that can be cited with sources well outside the Catholic Church.) The Catholic Church is being investigated on this score by state attorneys general; time will show whether this is because the Catholic Church has a visible structure that actually aids transparency (even when bishops don't want it to), or whether it's a down payment on major persecution of the Church by secular authorities.

Even brilliant and holy people can be fooled. Perpetrators of sexual abuse are often master manipulators. If they weren't, most of them would not have be able to commit the crimes they did. Legionaries of Christ founder Fr. Marcel Maciel fooled many, including Pope John Paul II. How? John Paul had been a priest and bishop for decades in communist Poland, where political leaders, under the thumb of Stalinist and early post-Stalinist Moscow, took Marxist atheist ideology seriously. They recognized the Catholic Church as a threat to their power. So they would frequently target priests—the best ones, not the worst, not the really guilty, and of course not those who were working for the secret police—with accusations of sexual vice. John Paul was used to this, perhaps too much so, and thus approached cases of alleged abuse skeptically. More generally, it is said that he had a tendency "to project his own virtues onto others." (See George Weigel, *Witness to Hope*, p. 470)

Not only the guilty suffer. The impact on innocent and faithful priests—the vast majority of them—remains tragic. Many report being shunned when people see the Roman collar. Suspicion makes the already difficult task of ministering to people's spiritual needs even harder.

How did the Catholic clerical abuse crisis even begin? First, temptation and sin are not new. In fact, the Church suffered from widespread clergy sexual immorality before, in the eleventh century. But why then did this terrible crisis of sin and corruption occur in this era? One explanation is that a more "liberal" attitude toward sexual morality in general was manifesting itself not only in society but also in seminaries. The sexual revolution reached a fever pitch in the sixties—but it had been raging for decades earlier, as documented by the Kinsey and Masters and Johnson reports. Academic moral theology does not take place in a vacuum. Young people don't like to hear—and older people don't like to teach—that the path to holiness requires sacrifices. The exception to this is when people "fall in love" with Christ and see his plan for them as liberating, not confining.

Many have blamed the current crisis on "clericalism." Though this term is at risk of becoming an all-purpose word for whatever the user doesn't like about the clergy or hierarchy, it does have a meaning. Clericalism is the notion that the clergy are a superior caste, that they are somehow what the Church is all about. Thus, clerical self-protection would be natural, and even commendable. The correct view would be that the clergy have a distinct role that is in service to the whole Church, laity included, indeed, laity foremost.

At the time of this writing, it is clear that the scandal of clergy sexual abuse is a worldwide phenomenon, but it's too early to

tell how the Church will emerge from this crisis and allow Christ
to cleanse it; we only trust that it will. In the meantime, we continue to do what we can to make amends to victims, prevent
abuse in all forms, and bring perpetrators and those who pro-
tect them to justice.

A Change of Age

Mike Aquilina

"Ours is not an age of change, but a change of age,"[1] Pope Francis observed shortly after his election to the papacy in 2013. It is one of the most quoted lines of his pontificate, and it does rather neatly capture the spirit of our time. As the second millennium wound down, the Church seemed to toll the bells for one epoch and yet eagerly anticipate the next. These were characteristic notes of the Second Vatican Council (1962–1965):

> Today, the human race is involved in a new stage of history. Profound and rapid changes are spreading by degrees around the whole world . . . . Hence we can already speak of a true cultural and social transformation, one which has repercussions on man's religious life as well.[2]

The same notes recurred through the pontificate of John Paul II, the last of the Council Fathers to occupy the chair of St. Peter. Elected in 1978, John Paul set his sights on the turn of the millennium, the year 2000. He began his 1994 document, *Tertio Millennio Adveniente* (*On the Coming Third Millennium*), with the suggestive biblical language of "the fullness of time."

The secular culture, meanwhile, was similarly moved by the seismic changes—and fascinated by the simultaneous change of decade, century, and millennium. But the secular response was different. It was anxious, and no one expressed the anxiety of the moment better than the pop musician Prince. Where the Church saw joy and hope, he saw only despair before an inevitable apocalypse. The Year 2000 meant the world was "out of time," and he called on listeners to party like it's 1999.

Other speculation presented other dreary alternatives for the future. The political scientist Francis Fukuyama, in his 1989 essay "The End of History," predicted a coming age of unrelenting and "certain boredom."[3]

The turn of the millennium came and went, and was followed soon afterward by the attacks by Islamist terrorists on the World Trade Center and the Pentagon. History failed to end on schedule. In fact, the overwhelming sense of change has persisted—and even intensified—within the Church.

Early in the new millennium, the Church in the United States endured a wave of scandals as news media reported allegations of widespread clergy sexual abuse. Lawsuits followed, and dioceses were forced into bankruptcy. As one attorney observed: "The zeitgeist is completely unfavorable to the Catholic Church."[4]

The scandals accelerated a sense of disenchantment in Catholics and non-Catholics. Fewer Americans and Europeans claimed any religious identity; on forms and in surveys they identify their religion as "None." Atheism and agnosticism made significant gains. As the culture shifted from modern to postmodern to post-Christian, the zeitgeist was increasingly unfavorable to tradition, authority, and the supernatural.

Even the people in the pews seemed tepid in their commitment. Polls showed that perhaps a majority rejected key doctrines, such as the real presence of Jesus in the Eucharist. St. John Paul's successor, Pope Benedict XVI, spoke of the Church's need to re-evangelize the baptized. Yet that was only the West. True, the West—and specifically Europe and North America—had been the site of history's most dramatic scenes in the second millennium. Today, however, the Church is growing most rapidly in the global South and East. Africa and India are sending priests to Europe and North America. And lands where the Church is harshly persecuted (China, Iran) are witnessing waves of conversion.

The rumors of history's end have proven to be exaggerated.

In the decade just past, the Church elected its first pope from the southern hemisphere—also the first Jesuit pope—following upon the extremely rare historic event of a pope's resignation. At every "change of age," churchmen propose the most ingenious remedies for Christianity's approaching catastrophes. In retrospect, the proposals often seem quaint. Man proposes; God disposes. And the Lord of History has resources that no observer—no historian, no political economist—can see. The catastrophes sometimes turn out to be the cure. We judge our times of persecution to be our golden ages of faith.

G. K. Chesterton observed that the Church often seems to be dying, and then rises again stronger than ever. It seems to be true. Imperial Rome slaughtered Christians by the thousand, but it was imperial Rome that fell to rubble while the Church went on to thrive. History should teach us to be uncertain about the shape of the future, but hopeful—and even confident—about its goodness. God's got this. The Lord of History has seen the end of history, and he has assured us that the powers of death, the gates of the netherworld, shall not prevail against his Church (see Matthew 16:18).

Notes

Chapter 1. The Modern Church

1. *Ineffabilis Deus*, http://www.newadvent.org/library/docs_pi09id.htm, viewed July 6, 2017. This declaration goes over the whole history of the doctrine.

2. The *Catholic Encyclopedia* defines the word as used in the term "Ecumenical Councils": "*Ecumenical Councils* are those to which the bishops, and others entitled to vote, are convoked from the whole world (*oikoumene*) under the presidency of the pope or his legates, and the decrees of which, having received papal confirmation, bind all Christians." http://www.newadvent.org/cathen/04423f.htm, viewed August 8, 2017.

3. Quoted in Chadwick, Owen, *A History of the Popes*, 1830-1914, Oxford: Oxford Univ. Press, 1998, repr. 2009, p. 207.

4. https://www.ewtn.com/library/councils/v1.htm#6, concluding paragraphs.

Chapter 2. Democracy and the "Social Question"

1. This war was causally linked to the loss of the Papal States. France, under her Second Empire, had been propping up the pope's vulnerable temporal domains. With the French army suddenly needed to defend the homeland against the Germans, it had to leave Italy.

2. http://www.newadvent.org/cathen/04168a.htm.

3. It may seem "existential Thomism" is an impossibility, because existentialism holds that "existence precedes essence," whereas for St. Thomas, essence, or being, has pride of place. If so, you're a "neo-Thomist" or a "Thomist of the Strict Observance." Welcome to the debate Leo made possible!

4. The first papal condemnation of enslavement of indigenous peoples was Eugenius IV's *Sicut Dudum*, 1435, fifty-seven years before Columbus's first voyage. Leo had issued bulls against slavery in 1888 and 1890. See https://www.catholic.com/magazine/online-edition/did-the-church-ever-support-slavery.

Chapter 3. A Crisis in Theology

1. The ordinary of the archdiocese has been called *patriarch* since the 1450s, after Venice was erected as an independent see in 1451.

2. https://www.thevintagenews.com/2017/03/17/st-marks-campanile-collapsed-in-1902-killing-no-one-except-the-caretakers-cat/.

3. Chiron, p. 116.

4. John Pollard, *The Papacy in the Age of Totalitarianism,* Oxford University Press, 2014, pp. 8-28.

5. *Ibid.,* 24mi.

Chapter 4. The War to End All Wars

1. https://www.thecatholicthing.org/2014/08/02/world-war-i-and-the-papacy/.

Chapter 5: Totalitarianism

1. The Aradi biography contains a photo of the Breithorn, in the French-Italian Alps, asserting that Fr. Ratti climbed it. There is also a picture of Ratti and several other snow-walkers traversing the Rothorn glacier in Switzerland in 1897. Ratti is in snow-boots, heavy jacket, fedora—and Roman collar.

2. http://query.nytimes.com/gst/abstract.html?res=9D02EED61130EE3ABC4F53D-FB4668389639EDE&legacy=true.

3. These details can be found in Volume 313 of *The Living Age,* starting at p. 17. https://books.google.com/books?id=cqk_AQAAMAAJ&pg=PA17&lpg=PA17&dq=the+irreconcilables+pius+xi&source=bl&ots=kL6s0ph3FX&sig=mmAlT7Ex-nZ2Rlg7Vzrm0iLsu0HE&hl=en&sa=X&ved=0ahUKEwj81qSPl93VAh-Viy1QKHXhGCr8Q6AEISjAE#v=onepage&q=the%20irreconcilables%20pius%20xi&f=false.

4. https://www.economist.com/blogs/freeexchange/2013/11/economic-history-1.

5. Years later he would refer back to this mission in his encyclical *Divini Redemptoris,* on Atheistic Communism, 1937.

6. "For if the nineteenth century was a century of individualism it may be expected that this will be the century of collectivism and hence the century of the State." From the article on fascism in the 1932 *Italian Encyclopedia,* attributed to Mussolini himself and his favorite contemporary political philosopher, Giovanni Gentile. http://sourcebooks.fordham.edu/mod/mussolini-fascism.asp.

7. Aradi, p. 149.

8. Aradi, p. 158.

9. Aradi, p. 161.

10. See Treaty: http://www.vaticanstate.va/content/dam/vaticanstate/documenti/leggi-e-decreti/Normative-Penali-e-Amministrative/LateranTreaty.pdf, Article 27, plus signatures.

11. Pius XI, *Non Abbiamo Bisogno,* para. 36.

12. "Hitler is recorded as saying that the German negotiators could agree to anything so long as the Concordat was signed. Later he could change or negate individual clauses." Pollard, *Papacy in the Age of Totalitarianism,* pp. 252-253. "As Pacelli bitterly remarked to the British minister at the Vatican shortly after the signing of the

Reichskonkordat. 'The Nazis probably would not violate all of the clauses of the Con-cordat at the same time.' By 1937, they had violated all the important ones." Pollard, pp. 266-267.

13. *Iniquis Afflictisque*, 26.

14. See e.g. Stanley G. Payne, *The Spanish Revolution*, New Yorker: W.W. Norton, 1970, ch. 1. Also, this article—https://en.wikipedia.org/wiki/Freemasonry_in_Spain—though sympathetic to Masonry, does a good job chronicling its development in Spain in tandem with Liberalism.

15. The Acton Institute estimates that approximately "6,800 priests, monks, nuns, and religious" were killed during and shortly before the Span-ish Civil War (1936–39). https://acton.org/publications/transatlantic/2017/11/06/remembering-martyrs-socialism-spanish-civil-war.

16. From the paragraph of his book, *The Common Law*, first published in 1881—but he served on the U.S. Supreme Court from 1902 to 1932.

17. https://books.google.com/books?id=Rq5hg4d54m4C&pg=PA120&lp-g=PA120&dq=lambeth+1930+Washington+Post+editorial&source=bl&ots=WKNog-2mwCn&sig=cXYxsSBs-QTgr7fm6Y-xZZCOvWw&hl=en&sa=X&ved=0ahUKEwjs-goXIuvHVAhUn7YMKHT3uAA4Q6AEIVjAH#v=onepage&q=lambeth%201930%20Washington%20Post%20editorial&f=false.

18. Pollard, p. 256.

19. Pollard, p. 278.

20. Excerpts concerning Jews and Judaism can be found at https://www.ccjr.us/dialogika-resources/primary-texts-from-the-history-of-the-relationship/hgu1938.

21. *The Hidden Encyclical of Pius XI* contains the "text" of "Humani Generis Uni-tas"—which can only mean it contains the Jesuit-drafted preliminary text, before Pius XI had a chance to review it. He used learned ghostwriters for most of his encycli-cals, but he always went over them carefully, deleting and adding. The Church in the 1930s fairly knocked herself out warning the world of the dangers of fascism and its racist baggage (and of communism too). Only the question of explicit condemnation of anti-Semitism remains. Bishops around the world protested the "Kristallnacht" pogrom in Germany in November, 1938. The Holocaust was still in the future, and still unthinkable.

22. Pollard, p. 288.

Chapter 6. World War II

1. Peter Barley, *Catholics Confronting Hitler*, San Francisco: Ignatius Press, 2016, p. 78.

2. https://www.britannica.com/biography/Pius-XII. Cardinal Merry del Val never became Pope, as he might have liked, but it's arguable that he trained a few. He is prob-ably the sub-Papal figure of the era most in need of a serious biography.

3. https://zenit.org/articles/1923-letter-shows-the-future-pius-xii-opposed-hitler/.

4. Ibid., citing Pinchas Lapide, *Three Popes and the Jews*, London: Souvenir Press, 1967, p. 121.

5. Rychlak, p. 121. Apparently Pius emphasized baptismal certificates. Papal biographer Yves Chiron, in his work on John XXIII thinks Roncalli in Ankara relied more on fake British immigration certificates from the Jewish Agency for Palestine. When the Israeli historian and diplomat Pinchas Lapide visited the newly-elected John XXIII to thank him for his efforts on behalf of Jews while he was Nuncio to Turkey, John averred that it was the Pope—Pius XII—who ordered such actions. On Lapide-John dialogue, see Pollard, *The Papacy in the Age of Totalitarianism, 1914-1958*, Oxford, 2014, p. 341.

6. See "'Pius XII saved thousands of Jews,'" Haaretz, July 7, 2010, reporting on findings to this effect by scholars at the Pave the Way Foundation and reported first by London's Daily Telegraph. http://www.haaretz.com/jewish/pope-pius-xii-saved-thousands-of-jews-1.300589.

7. Hans Gisevius, a Resistance leader and later a prosecution witness at Nuremberg, wrote: "The German Opposition was not a government competent to issue a binding signature to treaties or agreements. It, therefore, redounds greatly to the honor of the Pope that he, for the sake of European peace, put aside all misgivings and volunteered his services as a mediator." Hans Bernd Gisevius, *To the Bitter End: An Insider's Account of the Plot to Kill Hitler, 1933-1945*, 1947, repr. New York: Da Capo Press, 1998, p. 447.

8. Numerous recent authorities attest to Müller and his activities as described in Mark Liebling, *Church of Spies: The Pope's Secret War Against Hitler*, New York: Basic Books, 2015. See also Rychlak, *op.cit.*, and Thomas, *op.cit.*

9. Thomas, *The Pope's Jews*, p. 60.

10. Mark Riebling, *Church of Spies: the Pope's Secret War Against Hitler*, New York: Basic Books, 2015, p. 176.

11. Riebling, p 185, citing Owen Chadick, *Britain and the Vatican*, pp. 288-289, Sir Martin Gilbert, *The Righteous*, p. 314, and Susan Zachotti, *Under His Very Windows*, pp. 181-186, 200.

12. Michael Burleigh, *Sacred Causes*, p. 225.

13. Peter Hoffmann, *Carl Goerdeler and the Jewish Question*, Cambridge University Press, 2001, p. 102. As Mayor of Leipzing, 1934-37, Goerdeler refused to take down a statue of one of that city's favorite sons, Jewish composer Felix Mendelssohn, or to fly the swastika over city hall. Later he agreed that he would become Chancellor if the July 20 plot succeeded.

14. Liebling, p. 189.

15. Foa meeting and Goldmann letter, Thomas, *The Pope's Jews*, p. 67.

16. Thomas, *The Pope's Jews*, p. 67. On Pallottine Fathers, see ibid., p. 50.

17. Fr. Scavizzi's cause of beatification is moving forward. His ministry aboard the train was a project of the Knights of Malta. http://www.santiebeati.it/dettaglio/91721.

18. This is according to Fr. Scavizzi, as reported in Riebling, *Church of Spies,* p. 131. Fr. Scavizzi had put his observations in memo form and shown them to the Primate of Poland.

Chapter 7. The Cold War and Age of Benign Liberalism

1. Michael Burleigh, *Sacred Causes,* p. 320.

2. Ibid. p. 321.

3. Ibid. p. 320. The magnum opus on the transition from Nazi to Communist dictatorships is Anne Applebaum, *Iron Curtain: The Crushing of Eastern Europe, 1944–1956,* New York: Doubleday, 2012.

4. https://www.catholicnewsagency.com/news/hoax-or-history-the-communist-smearing-of-cardinal-stepinac-82848. See generally Esther Gitman, *When Courage Prevailed: The Rescue and Survival of Jews in the Independent State of Croatia, 1941–1945,* St. Paul, MN: Paragon House, 2011.

5. https://balkaninsight.com/2016/07/22/croatia-squashes-wwii-cardinal-stepinac-verdict-07-22-2016/.

6. Re Stepinac and Mindszenty, see Pollard, *The Papacy in the Age of Totalitarianism,* pp. 370-371.

7. Ibid. p, 258.

8. George Weigel, *Witness to Hope: The Biography of Pope John Paul II,* New York: Harper, 1999, p. 146.

Chapter 8. The Second Vatican Council

1. Jacques Chiron, *Jean XXIII,* p. 258.

2. Definition from the *Stanford Encyclopedia of Philosophy*: fideism is the doctrine "that faith is in some sense independent of, if not outright adversarial toward, reason." The same article lists condemnations of fideism by the Church, starting with Vatican I (which affirmed the rational knowability of God at the basic level of benign creator), through Pius X (*Pascendi* used the term "fideism" and considered it a form of Modernism) through John Paul II (*Fides et Ratio*) and Benedict XVI (*Caritatis in Veritate*). https://plato.stanford.edu/entries/fideism/.

3. See Benedict XVI, Christmas Address to the Roman Curia, December 22, 2005.

4. https://w2.vatican.va/content/paul-vi/it/audiences/1966/documents/hf_p-vi_aud_19660112.html Italian only: translation mine.

5. See e.g. https://www.ncronline.org/news/parish/new-spin-vatican-ii.

6. See e.g. https://rorate-caeli.blogspot.com/2017/07/the-myth-of-hermeneutic-of-continuity.html.

7. While the Latin Rite today is instantiated mainly in the two "forms" of the *Missale Romanum*—"Ordinary" (1970) almost always in the vernacular, and "Extraordinary"

(1962 or earlier) always in Latin; see *Summorum Pontificum*—other forms exist within the Latin Rite, which are particular to orders or to places.

8. Yves Chiron, *Annibale Bugnini, Reformer of the Liturgy,* Brooklyn, NY: Angelico Press, 2016, p. 93.

9. https://adoremus.org/1964/11/21/lumen-gentium/.

10. Expression attributed to Msgr. Robert Hugh Benson, Catholic convert, son of a (Protestant) Archbishop of Canterbury, author of the famous apocalyptic novel *Lord of the World*; this according to popular Catholic blogger Jeffrey Miller: http://www.splendoroftruth.com/curtjester/2008/05/show-i-stray-or-should-i-go/ I myself find it a little modern for turn-of-the-twentieth-century Benson, but it's possible.

11. https://www.vox.com/2018/10/17/17983566/russia-constantinople-ukraine-eastern-orthodox-schism-autocephaly.

12. https://www.hprweb.com/2014/06/decoding-vatican-iis-marian-paradigm-shift/.

13. Henri de Lubac, *Vatican Council Notebooks, Vol. 2,* San Francisco: Ignatius Press, 2016, p. 7; by "East" meaning, all but certainly, the Eastern Orthodox Churches.

Series Epilogue. A Change of Age

1. Pope Francis, informal address to the bishops of Brazil, July 27, 2013. He is, in fact, quoting a line from the 2007 "Aparecida Document," the final report of the Fifth General Assembly of the Bishops of Latin America and the Caribbean. Francis himself, then the Cardinal-archbishop of Buenos Aires, helped to draft the report.

2. Second Vatican Council, *Pastoral Constitution on the Church and the Modern World (Gaudium et Spes)*, 4.

3. Francis Fukuyama, *The End of History and the Last Man* (New York: Free Press, 1992), 330.

4. Bernard Condon and Jim Mustian, "Surge of New Abuse Claims Threatens Church Like Never Before," Associated Press, December 1, 2019.

For Further Reading

Barley, Peter. *Catholics Confronting Hitler.* San Francisco: Ignatius Press, 2016.

Chadwick, Owen. *A History of the Popes, 1830–1914.* Oxford: Oxford University Press, 1998, repr. 2009.

Gisevius, Hans Bernd. *To the Bitter End: An Insider's Account of the Plot to Kill Hitler, 1933–1945.* 1947. Reprint, New York: Da Capo Press, 1998.

Liebling, Mark. *Church of Spies: The Pope's Secret War against Hitler.* New York: Basic Books, 2015.

Lubac, Henri de. *Vatican Council Notebooks.* Vol. 2. San Francisco: Ignatius Press, 2016.

Marchione, Margherita. *Pius XII, Architect for Peace.* New York: Paulist Press, 2000.

Pollard, John. *The Papacy in the Age of Totalitarianism, 1914–1958.* Oxford: Oxford University Press, 2014.

Riebling, Mark. *Church of Spies: The Pope's Secret War against Hitler.* New York: Basic Books, 2015.

Weigel, George. *Witness to Hope: The Biography of Pope John Paul II.* New York: Harper, 1999.

Index

David M. Wagner is a lawyer and journalist who also works as a research fellow at the National Legal Foundation. He previously served as a law professor at Regent University, a speechwriter for the US Department of Justice, and as deputy counsel for the House Foreign Relations Subcommittee on International Operations and Human Rights.

Wagner earned his bachelor's and master's degrees from Yale University, where he specialized in theological and institutional Church history. He earned his law degree from George Mason University in 1992. He earned American Jurisprudence awards in 1989 and 1991. His work has appeared in publications including *First Things, National Catholic Register, Crisis, National Review, The Weekly Standard,* and *City Journal.* Wagner covered the 1985 Extraordinary Synod on Vatican II for *The Washington Times.* He also contributed to the book *Liberalism at the Crossroads.*

Wagner lives in the Washington, DC, area with his wife, Kathleen. They have five children and one grandchild.

Facebook: David M. Wagner
Twitter: @david_m_wagner

Mike Aquilina is a Catholic author, popular speaker, poet, and songwriter who serves as the executive vice president of the St. Paul Center for Biblical Theology.